# Vacation Homes
## and Perfect Weekend Hideaways

Karen Howes

# Vacation Homes
## and Perfect Weekend Hideaways

**MERRELL**
LONDON · NEW YORK

# Contents

# Introduction

If I didn't live in London, I should live a long way from civilization, perhaps on an island off the north-west coast of Scotland. For years I have dreamed of living in a lighthouse in which all the rooms are round, with a narrow widow's walkway at its pinnacle from which I could see far across the ocean. I have imagined myself standing there in the spray of waves that have travelled thousands of miles across the Atlantic. There is no telephone or internet connection. I am alone with nature in all its vicissitudes. For a change, I am not in control of my life. Yet I realize that I could not live like this all the time. It is the contrast with my other life that makes it so alluring.

Why do we seek alternatives to our daily experiences? Are we hoping to enter a dream universe, a place where we can act out fantasies that we barely acknowledge but that keep us sane? Modern city-dwellers live in a fast-paced world that is constantly changing, and many

seek to buy or rent properties in the countryside, where they can lead a different, less frenetic life for a weekend or a longer vacation. In addition, as more and more celebrities seek to acquire property in picturesque rural spots, there is more media focus than ever before on where and how we live.

There are numerous ways to find solace, comfort or challenge. Some people gravitate towards the mountains in pursuit of skiing or climbing adventures and other outdoor activities. Their ideal vacation homes and weekend hideaways would be set against a backdrop of snow-capped peaks, the rooms cosily furnished and warmed by roaring log fires.

Those who prefer the sea are drawn to the idea of a property perched on a cliff overlooking a vast expanse of ocean, or a simple cottage on a beach, where the rhythmic beating of the surf can

Opposite: *The Iveragh Peninsula of County Kerry extends into the Atlantic Ocean and is one of the remotest stretches of coastline in Europe. Extreme weather and high seas batter the cliffs (Cill Rialaig, page 218).*
Above: *A dhow returns to Lamu after a day's fishing in the Indian Ocean (Beach House, page 138).*

The dramatic pink living-room of Liza Bruce and Nicholas Alvis Vega's Jaipur apartment is furnished with sequinned mattresses and cushions covered in Art Deco-era saris (page 104).

restore a sense of life's priorities; these are places where children can play outside from dawn until dusk, where the ambience is generally warm and southern, and the emphasis is on al fresco meals and midnight swims.

Others love woodland and forests, places where they can feel truly 'buried' in the countryside. They favour misshapen architectural follies deep in bluebell woods frequented by foxes and badgers and the occasional intrepid walker, where evenings are spent chatting around the hearth amid a wealth of unread books. Such people are drawn to converted farmhouses in the folds of the Welsh hills, for example, where harsh weather can isolate you for days.

For those with a different sense of adventure, there are vacation homes and camps in the African bush, where life involves daily encounters with wild animals. Some inhabitants of Nairobi and

other big cities regularly flee to the hinterland, forsaking the urban bustle to immerse themselves for a weekend in beautiful countryside. No matter where we live, we will always need to escape and to rediscover our 'real' self.

Apart from the environment to which we are naturally drawn – whether its main feature is mountains, sea, forest or desert – the choice of vacation home is often influenced by friends and family who live in the area and may have introduced us to it. Then there are the buildings that 'speak' to us: a romantic ruin encountered while visiting a place for the first time, and which becomes the focus of a restoration dream; or an inherited property in which the next generation can act out its fantasies, a house laden with a sense of personal history, family heirlooms and gloomy ancestral portraits, its echoing corridors ringing with childhood memories.

*The path from Celia Lyttelton's Yorkshire cottage leads up to the moor and passes the ruin of a small stone piggery (Overwood, page 134).*

*Scatter cushions lie in the shade of an ancient fig tree in the garden of Sa Como Sequera in Majorca (page 16). The garden was originally designed by Cecil Beaton.*

Whether we seek to own or rent a second home, the idea of being involved with more than one property appeals to the romantic in us all. Our main home, where we are expected to behave responsibly and to fit in with social expectations, is closely interwoven with our working lives. By contrast, in the place where we spend our leisure time the sense of responsibility is diminished; there is no need to account for our time, and we can be whoever we choose to be at that moment, on that weekend. The second home is a place to which we can invite friends for whom we never seem to have enough time during the working week, and where we can spend hours setting the world to rights over supper in the kitchen.

Ownership of a second home, however, has its disadvantages: the property requires maintenance and, after progressive weekends of mowing lawns, cleaning gutters and preparing the

house for winter, can feel more like a burden than a joy. Weekends once filled with new discoveries and forays to local markets become occupied by chores, while the delight of eating home-grown vegetables is tempered by the hours spent weeding and pulling up produce that has failed to thrive in our absence.

For those of us who are reluctant to take on a weekend home, or for whom such an idea is an unaffordable luxury, unusual properties are increasingly available to rent for a week, or even a weekend, at a time. Instead of feeling obliged to spend all our free time in the same place, we can rent a cottage in Norfolk for a spring weekend and a villa in Tuscany for the summer vacation, accept an invitation to the exclusive island of Mustique for a winter pick-me-up, and finish the year skiing in Colorado.

*The swimming pool at the house on Majorca designed by Paco Muñoz looks out over the sparkling waters of the Mediterranean (Los Piños, page 144).*

*View from the terrace at the Beach House on Cape Agulhas in South Africa, where the Atlantic and Indian oceans meet in some of the continent's best fishing grounds (page 208).*

Fantasy is not restricted to ownership. A tiny bothy with a red corrugated-iron roof overlooking a sea loch on the Scottish island of Skye has become an inextricable part of my family's shared history. We are not regular visitors, but for a week every year or so – often in the bleakest of weathers – a stay at the bothy reawakens the new dimension that this place has brought to our lives. When my brother's twin daughters first visited Skye at the age of two, they believed that the island belonged to me; as far as they are concerned, the croft with whitewashed stone walls, protected by a rocky garden from the grazing Highland cattle, will forever remain one of several houses that I own on my island.

To disillusion my nieces would be to destroy the story. From climbing their first Munro on New Year's Day to a boat trip with my two dogs to the islands where seals like to sunbathe, from long

walks through steep-sided mountain valleys to beachcombing along the loch shore in all weathers, the two young girls have the experience of this corner of Scotland indelibly stamped on their imagination. Both children keep a handful of white Skye sand hidden in a drawer at home as a memento of a place where their spirits run free and to which their thoughts keep returning.

*One of the original cabins of the remote gold-mining village that has been transformed into the exclusive resort of Dunton Hot Springs, in the Colorado Rockies (page 120).*

# Vacation Homes

# Sa Como Sequera

## Majorca

SPAIN

Sa Como Sequera, or As You Like It, is an old finca (farmhouse), once the much-loved home of Chiquita Astor, isolated amid the rocky hills of Majorca. Purchased in 1969 at a knock-down price, the finca was partially restored in keeping with Majorcan tradition. Friends who came to stay were mainly painters and writers, longing for the solitude and peace that the finca offered, and prepared to put up with the lack of electricity and creature comforts in exchange for a bohemian lifestyle.

In those early days a regular visitor and source of constant encouragement was the photographer Cecil Beaton, who took on the design and devised the eventual colour scheme of the garden. With the help of an old military map of the area and the unpredictable expertise of a local water diviner, Beaton discovered vast reserves of water under the property, and his imagination was allowed free rein as the garden took shape. Against the backdrop of rock-strewn hills, pine trees and

scrub, Beaton created a lush oasis of green and grey tones, incorporating existing ancient trees, their gnarled shapes providing shade and points of interest around the property. For Chiquita Astor, the finca became the one place in which she could find the peace and privacy to indulge her passion for painting, but as her children grew up they ceased to visit, and eventually she was faced with the prospect of having to part with the property. The legacy of Beaton's work on the garden was still in evidence when a German couple chanced upon the house, although the strict division of colour had lost its definition, and the green-and-grey design had become confused. Yet there was still the startling and unexpected green of the lawn and the gentle hissing of sprinklers in a garden overwhelmed by a truly English combination of plumbago, honeysuckle, soft-pink roses and fruit-laden fig trees.

Pages 16–17: *Mimmi O'Connell has created a series of outdoor rooms and covered terraces.*
Opposite: *The kitchen door opens on to a terrace.*
Above, top left: *Candles and lanterns are kept in the sitting-room for those nights when the electricity fails.*
Above, top right: *A small writing-desk occupies one corner of the white master bedroom.*
Above, bottom left: *Sofas are upholstered in striped fabric from Sanderson and Ian Mankin.*
Above, bottom right: *Cushions of French mattress ticking are paired with a blue-and-white Indian dhurrie.*

Top left and right: *The Mediterranean-style kitchen is decorated with bright-blue-and-white French tiles in various patterns.*
Bottom left: *The former bread oven is now used for storing logs.*
Bottom right: *In the cloakroom, a Majorcan ceramic bowl has been transformed into a washbasin.*

Twenty years after she had first fallen in love with the finca, Chiquita sold up and moved on. The new era brought with it radical change, as the German couple embarked on some serious structural work. When this had been completed, including the installation of some interesting tiled floors, and furniture had been purchased from antiques shops around Europe, they sought the inspiration of an interior designer to pull all the elements of the house together. They found what they believed to be the right instinctive balance in the work of Mimmi O'Connell.

Mimmi's approach to creating harmony was to organize an invasion of artisans from London to paint, decorate and arrange every room and cupboard in the finca. The arrival of the workforce was swiftly followed by two container-loads of furniture, much of which was reupholstered in the signature striped fabric of the London designer Ian Mankin, a look that worked well with the white rough-plaster

*The white master bedroom, with its black-and-gilt wrought-iron bed frame, is one of the few rooms to be carpeted.*

walls and ironwork. Mimmi likes to employ the term 'subtle opulence' when designing houses in the country; this can be interpreted as the copious use of white on white, such as the combination of Sardinian embroidered carpets, Irish linen and mother-of-pearl-decorated duvets found in the various bedrooms. The most important room in the house was the kitchen, which became not only the main entrance but also the place to which family and guests naturally gravitated during the day.

A promise to Chiquita that Beaton's garden would be well looked after meant that an army of gardeners was kept busy replanting and maintaining what had been salvaged from the original design. For several years after the finca had been completed, the new owners could hardly bear to drag themselves away from it. However, they have now also moved on, perhaps with as lingering a backward glance as when Chiquita closed the front door for the last time.

# Vygekraal

## Robberg Peninsula
## Western Cape

SOUTH AFRICA

On a stretch of some of the most spectacular coast in South Africa, the line of dramatic and rugged cliffs that makes up the Robberg Peninsula, about 8 kilometres (5 miles) south of Plettenberg Bay, is broken by an extraordinary fairytale building. Perched on the cliff edge is an eccentric stone-built house masquerading as a crenellated castle.

Known locally as Vygekraal, the castle was built in the early 1960s by a civil engineer who was entranced by the beauty of the peninsula and its views over the Indian Ocean. Set in a private estate bounded by coastline, this magical building is surrounded by coastal *fynbos*, a form of vegetation unique to the region, in a nature reserve that the engineer created to ensure his privacy.

Twenty years later, the castle on the cliff caught the eye and the imagination of Serena Crawford, who fell in love with it. Within six months her wedding ceremony was conducted on the cliff, the first

Pages 22–23: *The imaginative folly with its series of terraces has unimpeded views over the Indian Ocean.* Above and opposite: *The living-room has picture windows opening to the sea. It is decorated almost entirely in blue and white, with fabrics from India and Malabar, Balinese textiles used as throws, and a large mirror in a driftwood frame.*

of many important family celebrations to be held there. Serena has since restored a succession of extraordinary and diverse properties in South Africa, Australia and England, but the castle has remained the single constant and is adored by her entire family.

It took a further twenty years to transform the castle into the ultimate vacation home: a long time by European and American standards, perhaps, but when the family were there on vacation they were having too much fun to take much notice of the builders; also, building projects in South Africa tend to take longer to complete because there is less sense of urgency. When the full extent of the roof problems and the damp damage was revealed, it became obvious that the engineer's vision had resulted in a folly that was no longer fit for human habitation. Most of the restoration work was orchestrated from Australia, where Serena was living, and from where she faxed pages of

*An Indian daybed sits at the foot of a simple cane bed in one of the comfortable guest bedrooms.*

instructions to local builders. Each time she returned to the castle after an absence, she would approach with a feeling of terror at what she might find had been done or 'improved', since the interpretation of her instructions was often alarmingly wide of the mark. Examples of the builders' creativity included a swimming pool in the middle of the drive, and beds that were so high off the ground that, rather than falling into bed, one had to launch oneself up on to the mattress!

Serena's decoration of the folly is based on the idea that any colour will do as long as it's blue. The rooms are filled with comfortable furniture, the predominant blue theme reflecting the views of the ocean through the large windows, and the emphasis is on creating a relaxed vacation atmosphere.

As a result of a second renovation, during which new bedrooms were added, Serena decided in the 1990s to make the castle available to like-minded families who were seeking a special place

in which to get away from it all. Her own family still begins to get excited in August at the prospect of spending time at the castle during the Christmas holidays, and now that her husband has retired, the couple can spend more time at this fabulous property at other times of the year. However, the castle is available for rent when the family is not in residence.

There must be no shortage of people waiting to put their name down to experience the vacation of a lifetime. From the living-room and open terraces of the castle, whales, dolphins and seals can be spotted in the ocean directly beneath, while a family of sea otters lives in the dam alongside the property. The unique protection afforded by the nature reserve has made the estate famous for birds: kestrels, black eagles, nectar feeders and a variety of seabirds are among the regular visitors.

Left: *The bathroom has a Victorian free-standing bathtub and Victorian washbasins.*
Top right: *Family photographs line both sides of a corridor.*
Bottom right: *The master bedroom has cane side tables and a cane sofa covered with a Balinese ikat.*

# Baholyodhin House

## Bangkok

THAILAND

The Anglo-Thai designer Ou Baholyodhin has a home in London: a penthouse in the famous Highpoint Two building, which, with its neighbour Highpoint One, towers over the city from its northern vantage point on Highgate Hill. Designed in the 1930s by the Russian-born architect Berthold Lubetkin for Sigmund Gestetner, the head of the Gestetner office-equipment firm, the buildings were intended as social housing for the firm's workers but were never used as such. Instead, all the apartments were reserved before completion by wealthy middle-class house-hunters.

The supposed antithesis to Ou's London life is a property in Bangkok. As creative director of the Thai Silk Company, Ou regularly commutes to Bangkok, where demanding schedules and an endless round of meetings and parties often leave him more exhausted than he is from his life in London. Ou was born in Thailand, however, and knows how to relax in a city such as Bangkok.

His home there is on a pocket of land that was bought by his grandparents on their marriage. Ou's mother now occupies the original house, his niece lives next door, and his uncle is building a home on the other side of the plot. Compared to his home in London, this one is more exotic and colourful. It does not need to be as functional, since Ou does not live there all year round, yet its familiarity is essential to him, and he sees it as a place where all his favourite possessions can co-exist in harmony.

For Ou, time at his Bangkok home is all about being close to his family. What he longs for on his return there is the familiar sense of well-being that he always feels as soon as he reaches the house. Bangkok's hectic bustle is shut out by the heavy gates to the compound, behind which he retreats to enjoy precious moments of peace. Within the compound is a pool surrounded by jungle

Opposite: *The swimming pool was designed by Ou to mirror the dimensions of the house.* Above, left: *Ou's workspace has a table that he designed for Gerald Pearce, an Arco lamp, chairs by Bertoia Diamond, and paintings by Erez Yardeni.* Above, top right: *A large white orchid offset by a velvet backdrop is paired with a small statue of Buddha, graced with fresh jasmine, on a tabletop.* Above, bottom right: *Sofas of Thai silk and a coffee table and sideboard designed by Ou adorn the sitting-room.*

greenery. Here Ou takes his daily swim, often early in the morning before leaving for work, followed by a massage from his mother's visiting masseur, during which he catches up on the local gossip and everything else he has missed since his last visit. His favourite moment is when – whatever the weather – he steps into the outdoor shower.

Ou's house was designed by the German architect Stefan Schlau to promote a calm and simple way of life. The ground-floor living and study area has plenty of space to accommodate Ou's favourite range of furniture, most of which he designed for Gerald Pearce, the owner of the Thai Silk Company. An open-plan bedroom is above it. By contemporary European standards, the house cost next to nothing to build; the addition of the outdoor swimming pool, which mirrors the dimensions of the house to ensure spatial harmony, brought the cost of the property up to £25,000.

Inside, Ou has added a careful choice of collectable items. Buddha statuettes and antique textiles, bought during trips to Myanmar (Burma) and Indonesia, have found a home in the bedroom; the ground-floor room, permeated by the scent of jasmine from the garden, is decorated with some of his grandfather's sculptures.

These intimate family surroundings help Ou to feel grounded during his visits to Bangkok. While he currently lives in England, he acknowledges that he is unlikely to stay there forever. Successive generations of his family have put down roots in Bangkok, so he is reassured that the house, and the sense of belonging somewhere, will always remain.

Below: *The green silk bedcover in the bedroom is available through Jim Thompson. An antique Thai textile hangs on the wall.*
Opposite: *The large outdoor shower is flanked by plants and used throughout the year.*

# The Glen

## Jura

SCOTLAND

The Isle of Jura, the third-largest of Argyll's islands, and part of the Inner Hebrides, is situated off the west coast of Scotland. Reputedly the wildest, emptiest and least visited of Britain's inhabited islands, Jura has a population of barely two hundred, who share its moorland, beaches and trout-filled lochs with more than six thousand deer; the name Jura derives from the Norse word for Deer Island.

Dominating the island's skyline are the scree-covered Paps, three steep conical mountains that rise to a height of nearly 800 metres (2600 feet) and stand sentinel over this wild, remote and beautiful part of Scotland. They are called Beinn an Oir (the Mountain of Gold), Beinn Shiantaidh (the Sacred Mountain) and Beinn a' Chaolais (the Mountain of Sound).

The island has six private estates, one of which has been in the Astor family for more than a century. The Astor estate includes a bothy that is known by the family as The Glen and sits in the centre of a

bay, against a spectacular backdrop of the Paps. Beyond the wall enclosing the garden stretches the beach and then the sea, with views to the island of Colonsay, more than 16 kilometres (10 miles) distant.

The Glen was built in the 1850s, when Jura's population was several times greater than it is today. The bothy would have served as an occasional dwelling, with a nearby stable for ponies – the only means of transport at the time – providing additional shelter for deerstalkers as the sport became more popular. In its original form, it consisted of three cottages; when Annabel Astor and her husband, William, took on the property in the 1980s, they knocked the three buildings into one. It was sparsely furnished with pieces brought down from the main house, and running water was obtained via a small hand pump, which brought water from the Batrick, a nearby stream. When the pump broke – a regular occurrence, it seems – they resorted to bringing water down by bucket.

Opposite: *A wonderful family retreat on the west coast of Scotland, The Glen stands in its own bay looking out over the Atlantic Ocean.*
Above: *Engravings by Edwin Landseer hang on the matchboarded walls of the sitting-room. Annabel Astor created the cornice of scallop shells, and blankets from the Islay Woollen Mill hang over the arms of the chairs and sofa.*

Above, left: *Wide views of the coast and countryside can be enjoyed from the sitting-room window.*
Above, top right: *A corner of the sitting-room is hung with a collection of watercolour seascapes.*
Above, bottom right: *In the kitchen, fruit is stored in labelled baskets, which are hung high on the wall, out of the reach of mice.*
Opposite: *Sue Jones created the fabulously ornate, shell-encrusted chimney-piece and mirror frame that dominate the small sitting-room.*

An indoor bathroom and an oil-fired boiler have since replaced the antediluvian arrangements, and provide both a practical means of drying sodden clothing and a source of hot water. Candles and hurricane lamps, which had been the only form of lighting for the first ten years, were replaced by gas lamps; although the gentle hissing of the gas lamps was wonderfully atmospheric, they were essentially impractical, with spare parts almost impossible to obtain. In due course The Glen switched to electricity, and the gas lamps were all converted.

Over the years the bothy has evolved into a wonderful, cosy family retreat. For practical reasons, since there is no central heating and the approach by boat is dependent on benign weather conditions, it is used only in summer. During this time, routine repairs and maintenance have to be carried out, for which family and friends are regularly roped in. After a bleak winter, The Glen takes

*Annabel's bedroom also has a chimney-piece designed with shells by Sue Jones.*

several weeks to get up and running, and at the end of every summer there is a strict routine for shutting it down. Anything likely to fall victim to damp or pest attack is hung from the ceiling, while the mice take over at ground level. Sand blows in through the cracks in the walls and under the doors, and the walls have been known to run with damp. The roof needs to be repaired after every winter, and the door- and window frames tend to warp and break. Oil has to be ordered and then brought out by boat in jerrycans and hauled up the beach, along with sacks of coal and other essentials. Shopping involves a weekly expedition to Islay (which, although less than two kilometres [about a mile] away, is connected to Jura only by ferry), so life has to be carefully planned.

The family goes to Jura every summer. For Annabel, whose life involves maintaining a successful business in London and a great deal of foreign travel, the island offers an important

respite. Lost in the spectacular landscape of her summer home, she likes to be reminded of humanity's insignificance, a feeling reinforced by the extremes of weather in the bay, where storms are spectacular and violent, throwing up a dark sky against the fine white coral sand and its contrasting riot of green and red seaweed.

Annabel looks forward to being woken by the squabbling of gulls and the sound of the waves sucking at the beach. If she is lucky, she might catch sight of a sea otter swimming across the bay, rolling gracefully on to its back. At high tide, in the company of her three Jack Russell terriers, she often takes the rubber dinghy out to the string of rocks in the bay and talks to the grey seals, which swim around the boat, baiting the dogs. At other times, family members take the boat out to deeper water and go mackerel fishing, or tempt the sea trout in the small river beside the bothy.

Left: *The walls of a cosy and comfortable guest bedroom are lined with fabric.*
Top right: *Pine cladding preserves the rustic feel of this small bathroom.*
Bottom right: *A second bathroom provides a warm place in which to dry clothes.*

# Casa Cadaqués

## Cadaqués · Costa Brava

SPAIN

Many years ago, before the tourist boom hit Spain, the coastal resorts that have become notorious for their high-rise hotels and packed beaches consisted of a series of small, picturesque fishing villages with occasionally a swimmer or a child paddling along the water's edge searching for cowrie shells. Only a handful of families would visit the beach for the day, perhaps exchanging words with one of the Guardia Civil officers who regularly patrolled the shoreline. Otherwise the coast would be deserted.

Cadaqués, on Spain's rugged Costa Brava, two hours' drive north of Barcelona, was in those days a tiny fishing village. It was a favourite haunt of Picasso, Matisse and Marcel Duchamp, all of whom came to the village to paint and to relax. Although perhaps less wild than it was then, the village still retains the rakish air of an artists' colony; it is accessible only by a hazardous, winding

mountain road, which descends from the foothills of the Pyrenees to the Mediterranean. Peter Dunham, a designer from Los Angeles, cannot remember a time when he did not go to Cadaqués for his holidays.

Peter's bohemian parents first discovered the village in the early 1960s and with it a centuries-old fieldstone hut, which stood alone on a rocky, windswept promontory overlooking the bay. Although the hut was isolated from the village and without electricity and running water – there was just an old cistern in which rain collected – the Dunhams and a group of like-minded fellow Americans decided to pool their resources and buy it. With the proprietor of the local café acting as building manager, the hut was restored and modernized, and a semicircle of rooms was added, all facing the sea. The simple peasant architecture – rough whitewashed walls,

Left: *The house stands on a remote and rugged promontory on Spain's Costa Brava, where Peter has spent every summer since early childhood.*
Above: *Lazy summer days are whiled away on the split-level terrace in the shade of the olive trees.*

terracotta floors and a red-tiled roof – is typical of the area and belies the difficulties the Dunhams experienced in the property's reconstruction. With no access to Cadaqués by land except along a goat track over the hills, all the building materials had to be brought by boat and hauled up to the site by donkeys.

During Peter's childhood, the newly extended property resembled a makeshift family summer camp. One of the buildings served as the kitchen, another was divided into bedrooms, and the third housed the overflow of children and nannies; sometimes there would be as many as twelve children sleeping in one room. There was no living-room as such, and everyone lived out of doors, getting up with the sun and finishing dinner by candlelight, the children roaming free while the adults relaxed, played cards and set the world to rights.

Opposite: *Local flowers have been hung to dry from the rafters in a sociable corner of the rough-plastered living area.*

Above: *Traditional Mediterranean-blue paint brightens the furniture as well as the window frame in the whitewashed kitchen.*

*The sofas and built-in plaster furniture in the sitting-room are covered with colourful Uzbekistani susanis and Indian block prints.*

Peter remembers leaving the car near Salvador Dalí's house in the village and piling groceries, friends and all the essentials for the stay into a boat for the twenty-minute ride to their landing. Everything would then have to be carried up the steep flight of steps carved into the cliff. As the years went by, some of the couples began to drop out, and Peter's parents gradually bought up their shares, until eventually they felt it was time for Peter himself to take over the property.

Reluctant to change the essential soul of a place so full of happy childhood memories, Peter made a few necessary improvements to its basic comforts, replaced the battered US Army beds with built-in plastered furniture, and covered the old sofas and beds with colourful susanis from Uzbekistan and Indian block-print fabrics. He also added an outdoor shower and cold running water, but drew the line at installing electricity or a telephone. Too much civilization would have destroyed the magic.

Peter continues to visit the summer home of his childhood, and tries to spend at least three weeks there every year. Careful about the friends he invites to share this special existence, he admits that the rudimentary facilities do not satisfy everyone. For Peter, however, there is nothing in the world that affords him more pleasure than the first swim at Cadaqués after he wakes to the sound of the waves breaking on the rocks beneath his bedroom. He considers this to be the single greatest luxury of his life.

*This simple bed was created by mounting a mattress on a plaster base; the mosquito netting is decorative as well as functional.*

# Ocean View

## Mustique

ST VINCENT AND THE GRENADINES

The ultimate luxury holiday destination is usually portrayed as a sun-drenched island surrounded by warm, azure-blue waters and endless stretches of bone-white, deserted sandy beaches: a description that fits the Caribbean island of Mustique perfectly. To the handful of people who are privileged to own a property on Mustique, it is quite simply paradise.

Mustique is what it is today thanks to the dream of Colin Tennant (Lord Glenconner), who bought the island in 1958, when the profitable trade from the sugar plantations of the eighteenth century had long since collapsed. At the time Mustique had no water and little working infrastructure. Since then Lord Glenconner has created a new village and set out to improve the basic living standards of the islanders. By the late 1960s Mustique was producing sea-island cotton, and the Mustique Company had been established to protect the island's interests. Lord

Glenconner's circle of close friends was intrigued by the secrecy surrounding his beautiful island, and it was not long before the international jet-set began to arrive. Mustique has been a favourite destination for wealthy lotus-eaters ever since.

The theatrical designer Oliver Messel, who had already established a reputation on the neighbouring island of Barbados for his imaginative properties in coral stone, collaborated with the architect Arne Hasselquist to build a series of secluded villas on Mustique, strategically scattered around the island to ensure maximum privacy. There are no proper roads on Mustique; each villa is located in its own piece of natural wilderness, where tortoises roam freely. An agreement was drawn up restricting the number of villas to 120, thereby safeguarding the island's rugged, natural beauty for future generations. The island has now reached its full quota of bespoke villas, and existing

Opposite: *Sun loungers and a gazebo for dining are positioned to overlook the infinity-edged pool.*
Above, left: *At night, the gazebo and swimming-pool terrace are lit with an abundance of lanterns.*
Above, right: *One of the terraces that surround the villa and overlook the gardens makes an alternative covered dining area.*

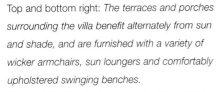

Top and bottom right: *The terraces and porches surrounding the villa benefit alternately from sun and shade, and are furnished with a variety of wicker armchairs, sun loungers and comfortably upholstered swinging benches.*
Bottom left: *The villa is approached by a flight of coral-stone steps.*

properties rarely come on to the market. Those who fall under the island's spell and wish to buy into the dream are subjected to a strenuous vetting by the Mustique Company to check their financial and social suitability, and, if found acceptable, may wait years for a house to become available.

Situated on one of the two highest points of the island, overlooking Mustique's small harbour, is a spectacular villa with views over the Caribbean. The light trade winds preclude the need for air conditioning and are sufficient to discourage mosquitoes. Unusually, the property existed only as a concrete shell when it was put up for sale. Its utilities were *in situ* and a floor plan of the rooms had been devised, but that was it. It took barely eight months for the villa to take shape, at the same time as guest cottages in the terraced garden were built and the garden was landscaped. The poolside gazebo, where family members spent most of their time, was the final touch of inspiration.

Although the villa was not constructed to her plan, the final design suited the owner and her family well, and she was happy to stay on her own in the completely self-contained main house. Furnishing a holiday home can be an endless source of pleasure, particularly for someone who travels extensively, and the result was an eclectic mix of furniture from Myanmar and Thailand, wicker from New York, Caribbean mahogany and the clever use of simple textiles. Any islander, from the Shetlands to the Caribbean, acknowledges a shared problem: salt water is no respecter of property; curtains and soft furnishings have to be replaced regularly and materials need to be hard-wearing. Consequently, the artwork that decorated the walls of the villa was chosen for colour and content rather than value.

The family spent most of their days outdoors. Breakfast on one of the many terraces that surround the villa was often followed by a lazy picnic lunch on the beach, just a few minutes' walk

*A spectacular octagonal entrance hall leads through into a central courtyard, which overlooks the swimming pool and the ocean beyond.*

away. Afternoons were whiled away with an apparently endless choice of pastimes, including a round of golf on a neighbouring island, tennis, horse riding, fishing or diving on the coral reef.

Mustique's one small town includes Basil's Bar and Restaurant, which is as famous for being the only place to stay on the island as it is for the food it serves. Otherwise, the residents entertain at home, and, following their afternoon of sport, return to their terraces and poolside gazebos to enjoy a sundowner and a good book before considering the next day's strenuous programme!

Opposite, clockwise from top left: *Oriental tables and sofas adorn the veranda; the dining-room has furniture in French 1940s style by Armini; the living-room coffee table is in burnt wood and glass by Ingrid St Donat; upholstery is in bright African batik.* Above, clockwise from left: *An Anglo-Indian antique mahogany daybed sits at the foot of a four-poster; another four-poster bed is decorated with Nigerian cushions; this room's theme was inspired by the 1930s design of the Jean-Michel Frank wall lights.*

# Brooke Cabin

## Nanyuki

KENYA

In 1947, when he was five years old, Timothy Brooke emigrated with his family to Kenya. On arrival in Nairobi, the family moved into a coffee manager's house and Timothy was sent to school at a Catholic mission, where he spent his formative years. Inheriting the interests of his father and grandfather, both of whom were amateur painters, Timothy never doubted that he would become an artist, but the small amount of instruction that he received in art at the Nairobi mission left him restless. In his late teens, he was sent to Europe on a one-way ticket with insufficient funds to pay for his return to Kenya, and he spent the next few years wandering around Paris, studying at an art college in England and becoming involved in an advertising agency in London. He then spent several years in Ireland, painting and living from hand to mouth, adapting easily to the independence and lack of convention, which reminded him of life in Kenya.

Page 50: *Sited between the Liki and Nanyuki rivers, the simple wooden cabin is almost engulfed by olive trees and undergrowth. Its roof is of corrugated iron, so the noise is deafening when it rains.*

Previous page: *This sunlit corner of the sitting-room looks out on to the terrace.*

Above: *The kitchen leads off the main living area, which is dominated by a circular table; the cedar-plank walls are covered with a map, notes, cards, mementos and newspaper cuttings, while Timothy's guitar hangs from a convenient nail.*

In the mid-1970s Timothy returned to Kenya and set off on one of his regular one-man safaris, living out of the back of a Land Rover. Heading north out of Nairobi, he drove through the highland area of the Aberdare Mountains and on past Mount Kenya, Africa's second-highest mountain. Reviving his love of the old, and in many cases abandoned, farmsteads dating back to the early twentieth century, when the area had first been discovered by European settlers, Timothy began to look around, considering the possibility of putting down roots, and found an old woman who was prepared to sell her property in Nanyuki. As things turned out, friends of his bought the house and he bought half the land. He then went back to Ireland, only returning to Kenya some eight years later.

Timothy's plot of land is at the end of Lunatic Lane, a dirt road flanked by market stalls and shabby hotels and bars. According to local legend, the otherwise unremarkable street

was named after an eccentric European woman who was seen on more than one occasion running naked down the track and screaming, imagining her husband to be in hot pursuit and wielding a carving knife.

Timothy's simple wooden house was built between the Liki and Nanyuki rivers, which run through his plot, with the help of a local man and his son. Measuring barely 10 × 5 metres (33 × 16 feet) in its original design, the cabin has a frame made of cypress embedded into a cement base, bolted together and clad in planks of cedar, the only wood in Kenya that is termite-resistant. Windows were cut out of the panels and hinged. Left open during the day, they allow in every sound and nuance of the outdoors, but at night they are firmly bolted against the threat of wild animals.

Left: *The compact kitchen is as orderly as a ship's galley, even though it contains an enormous number of objects; these have either been hung from hooks in the wooden rafters or nailed to the cedar planking of the walls.*
Top right: *Timothy stores his fishing tackle on the sitting-room wall; the nets hang from the ceiling. The zebra skin was bought locally many years ago, when it was still possible to acquire such skins.*
Bottom right: *The wall of Timothy's studio is daubed with many different colours of paint.*

*Just off the sitting-room is a bunk bedroom reached through a low doorway. The steps on the right lead up into the main living area.*

The sense of impermanence evoked by Timothy's wooden cabin required a few amendments when he met his future wife, Jill, and at her insistence they added a small sitting-room to enable them to enjoy open fires on chilly evenings. The cabin was extended by a few metres, and a new end wall, where the chimney would go, was constructed out of river stones. A lean-to bedroom soon followed. Until he built a separate studio a short walk away, Timothy would paint in a corner of the cabin. Storage space is at a premium there, and every item has its own special place, reminiscent of life on board ship.

Timothy has created at Nanyuki his own personal artist's retreat. Although purists might object to the presence these days of both water and electricity, at an altitude of 1500 metres (5000 feet) a hot shower is more than welcome on cold evenings, and electric lights are a lot less hazardous than

the original paraffin lamps. Drawn back to Kenya by the quality of light, which is at its best in the early morning, Timothy often spends time at the cabin on his own. He rises early, paints for part of the day and then passes the remainder of the afternoon either trout-fishing or watching the game on one of the nearby ranches. His strong, simple compositions draw on childhood memories in a country that continues to influence and inspire him.

Top left: *The bathtub is located in the undergrowth outside the cabin.*
Bottom left: *Interesting items on the terrace include a pair of wagon wheels and a bench salvaged from a builder's yard near Nairobi.*
Right: *The old-fashioned lavatory occupies a corner of Timothy's studio.*

# Methodist Cottage

## Shelter Island
## New York

USA

As New Yorkers flee their city on Friday evenings, and the freeways of Long Island and New Jersey clog up with tailgating cars heading out to the Hamptons and other popular weekend destinations, they leave behind a little-known jewel. There is an island that is ignored by those departing weekly from Manhattan, yet close enough to attract New Yorkers who prefer a more low-key weekend, isolated from the people with whom they tend to fraternize during the week.

Shelter Island measures 8 × 14 kilometres (5 × 9 miles), and is located between the North Fork and South Fork of Long Island, with Gardiner's Island, one of the largest privately owned islands in the United States, on the seaward side. The oldest settlement dates back to 1722, when Quakers persecuted by Puritans sought refuge there. In 1890 a Methodist summer camp was designed and built on the heights of Shelter Island by Calvert Vaux, who was also responsible for designing Central

Park in New York City. The camp consisted of sixty board-and-batten summer cottages, four parks, a prayer chapel, and a meeting- and dining-hall.

Shelter Island Heights now numbers 120 vacation houses dating from the late nineteenth century, and has been designated a National Historic District, where not even a wood-burning fireplace is permitted. This regulation ensures that Shelter Island remains primarily a summer location, since the clapboard construction of most of the island's properties means that they are generally too cold for winter habitation.

Joanne Creveling spent many childhood summers staying with her grandparents on the North Fork of Long Island, and remembers Shelter Island as an enchanted garden, completely surrounded by water. She would paddle a canoe or row out to it, in true *Swallows and Amazons* fashion, and

Opposite: *The nineteenth-century Methodist board-and-batten summer cottage, with its unassuming exterior, was the last in the community to be built.* Above, clockwise from left: *The porch's screens allow a breeze on hot summer days, but are fine enough to keep out mosquitoes, and blankets courtesy of Lufthansa hang over the backs of the chairs; the open porch is decorated with an unfurled US flag; most of the furniture in the cottage has been painted in the same milky white as the house itself.*

Above: *The library walls are hung with engravings
taken from an eighteenth-century encyclopaedia.*
Opposite, top left: *The screened-in porch shares
a window with the more formal living-room.*
Opposite, top right: *A rustic chair is set against
a wall of engravings in the library.*
Opposite, bottom left: *Ceramic objects make an
interesting group in a corner of the bedroom.*
Opposite, bottom right: *The porch is connected
to the cottage by a flight of steps.*

play along its shoreline. After an absence of twenty years, Joanne returned to Shelter Island one weekend with her husband, Frank, and her two young sons, and as they boarded the ferry she remembers experiencing a strange sense of belonging. The purchase of a Methodist clapboard cottage was the result, and so began years of idyllic summer vacations.

The cottage was white with black shutters and had a myriad tiny rooms crammed full of furniture, with thick 'over-curtains', 'under-curtains', blinds and draperies to keep out the light. The family spent their first summer tearing down the curtains and sorting through the 'inherited' furniture. Each weekend was like a treasure hunt, offering the excitement of finding cupboards within cupboards, mirrors inside wardrobes, and sundry objects stacked in kitchen cabinets. The unwanted discoveries were traded at flea markets for more appropriate items, while Joanne

Above, top left and bottom left: *The beds and night-stand in the guest bedroom were inherited with the cottage.*

Above, top right: *The removal of several walls opened up some of the rooms; the master bedroom, for example, now stretches the width of the cottage.*

Above, bottom right: *The small bathroom is full of mirrors, which were found at the cottage.*

Opposite: *The chaise-longue, love seat and bed in this bedroom are covered with white embroidered cloths; the cotton hemp rug was found in Paris.*

knocked down a few interior walls to create a sense of space and light. She banned dark colours, and the dirty browns, greys and greens of the original interior were soon replaced with a milky white; 140 litres (30 gallons) of paint later, every stick of furniture in the cottage had been painted to match the floors and walls. The clapboard exterior was painted misty silver, a colour that reflected the spruce trees and bamboo in the garden.

Having achieved the restful monochrome look on which she had set her heart, Joanne settled down to enjoy the peace and quiet of the island and the luxury of being able to do her own thing: the complete antithesis of a hectic life in New York City. On Shelter Island, where there is no cinema, no disco, no excitement other than from newspaper headlines, and where the lack of a late-night ferry service deters would-be revellers, life is allowed to run at its own pace.

# Goutal House

## Île de Ré
## Charente-Maritime

FRANCE

Île de Ré is a small island in the Atlantic off the coast of La Rochelle in western France. It is a combination of salt flats and long, silvery beaches, loved by locals and visitors alike for its luminous light and invigorating sea air, permeated by the smell of the pine trees that grow along the shoreline.

French perfumer Camille Goutal has been coming to Île de Ré for more than twenty years, ever since her mother, Annick, and stepfather, Alain Meunier, discovered the small house down a narrow *venelle* (alleyway) in one of the handful of pretty villages on the island, and chose it as their vacation home. It would appear to have been love at first sight. Peeking over the wall of the property, Camille's mother looked into the neglected courtyard and knew in a second that this was the house they should buy. The property changed hands without the couple even having bothered to look inside it.

Like the courtyard, the house had been sadly neglected, and much had to be done to put it in order. Before starting the restoration work, Annick and Alain visited the island every fortnight for several months to watch the effects of light on the building and monitor the trajectory of the sun during the different seasons. They decided to add an extra floor to the house, positioning the windows and sun terrace to take full advantage of the light, and installing a set of glass doors on the ground floor. The interior was then panelled by a local carpenter and the house furnished with antiques and quirky pieces from flea markets all over France. The pine-clad walls in the cosy living-room are hung with an array of seascapes, and painted shelves groan with books to help while away the long hot days of summer.

The all-important courtyard was planted with an olive tree, hydrangeas, roses and wisteria as well as hollyhocks, which are prolific on the island. The terrace is at its best during the afternoon,

Opposite: *The village of St Martin de Ré is centred on the quiet harbour.*
Above: *The bookshelves in the living-room are Camille's only addition to her mother's original design for the room.*

and as the sun moves around the house the courtyard below fills with evening sunlight, just in time for an aperitif.

During their childhood Camille and her stepsister, Charlotte, spent every holiday on the island, which has always held an important place in the heart of the family. Where today there is a bridge, in those early years they would wait for the ferry to transport them the short distance from La Rochelle to Île de Ré. They would spend their time cycling, swimming and lazing around, and the young Camille was taught by her mother to smell and appreciate the scent of everything on the island. The small house was always full of friends, and the girls slept in a tiny cottage across the courtyard. To accommodate an increasing number of visitors, Camille recently bought the old garage that once belonged to the property, immediately across the alleyway. It is tiny, like the original house, and shares its unique atmosphere. The extra space means that different members of the family can spend time there together, yet still have some privacy.

Camille and Charlotte both have children of their own now, and they continue to visit the house as often as possible. Since Camille's mother died in 1999, the family's vacation home, where they had enjoyed so many happy, carefree days, has taken on an additional significance. Although it is not lived in all year round, Camille tries to spend at least one long weekend every month at the house, and she meets her stepfather and other family members and friends there during the long summer vacation. She likes to be able to pick up the threads of her last visit immediately on her return.

A solitary person by nature, Camille loves to stay on the island out of season, when the summer visitors have left. She enjoys long walks on the beach, when the wind blows in from the Atlantic,

*The painted pine cabinets in the kitchen were made locally to Annick Goutal's design. The cooking range is by La Cornue.*

bringing with it a distinctive salty tang, and the autumn light, which has drawn artists to Île de Ré over the centuries, is reflected in the pools of shallow water left by the receding tide. With no jagged cliffs, the landscape is more benign than threatening, yet Camille always experiences a sense of wildness and freedom each time she returns to the island. Île de Ré may not be the most beautiful place in France, but Camille has never felt so much at home anywhere else, nor experienced the same sense of well-being.

Top left: *Camille's bicycle is propped outside in the alley, against the garage she recently bought.*
Top right: *The sun terrace, with its enormous painting, has views over the village.*
Bottom left: *Various artworks have been given to Annick and Alain over the years by artist friends.*
Bottom right: *Upstairs, in the bedrooms, the pine has been left unpainted.*

# Whaledance

## Kommetjie
## Western Cape

SOUTH AFRICA

How many people can claim to have seen a group of at least seventeen whales in the bay beyond the house they are building? It was a glorious event in itself, but the fact that one of the whales appeared to be dancing for its companions led to this South African beach house, which overlooks Hout Bay, being given the name Whaledance.

Now considered a suburb of Cape Town, Kommetjie, where Sheila Boardman chose to build her vacation home, was once a lobster-fishing village halfway around the coast of the Cape Peninsula, with Table Mountain as a backdrop, and surrounded by the Cape Peninsula National Park. One of those places that supposedly never changes, it has attracted artists and environmentalists for many years, and, more recently, surfers and wealthy weekenders. Its name (meaning 'Little Bowl') derives from the natural basin carved out of the rocky inlet by which it

Pages 66–67: *The beach house at Kommetjie was designed to take advantage of a unique ecological environment abundant with wildlife.*
Above: *The bookcase in the sitting-room was designed by Sheila Boardman to complement the cupboard doors and wall panelling. The beach-style furniture is upholstered in hard-wearing, casual fabrics.*
Opposite: *The simple, fluid staircase was created by designer Margie Walsh.*

stands, and which is surrounded almost entirely by a ridge of boulders, forming a perfect harbour for small boats.

There are now few places in the world where planning permission would be given for a new house on one of the most beautiful beaches in existence. Whaledance, though, is on one of the longest, widest and most beautiful stretches of beach in the Cape. Known as Long Beach, it extends for more than 8 kilometres (5 miles) from Kommetjie to Noordhoek. The sea here is too dangerous for swimming, but the northern end of the beach, known as 'the Hook', is a favourite place for surfing. The beach is popular with walkers, and when the waves are high in winter a lagoon forms in front of the dunes.

Apart from rare whale-sightings, seabirds are the main attraction along this coast. Friends and family would join Tom and Sheila Boardman on the teak deck around the swimming pool

Top left: *All the plates in this group are the work of the potter Hylton Nel.*

Bottom left and right: *The kitchen is completely open to the dining-room, which has spectacular views through three sets of French windows over Hout Bay.*

at Whaledance to watch the oystercatchers, terns, gulls and cormorants flying in to land on the nearby estuary.

Sheila had always intended to make her new house subordinate to the spectacular landscape. She had the clapboard exterior painted grey so that it would blend in with the sand; as it has weathered, the house has picked up the colours of the sea and mountain backdrop, so that it appears to float on the sand dunes. Every detail has been meticulously considered and executed, to the point of removing and replacing a sand dune, in itself quite a feat of engineering.

The former owner of a successful antiques shop in Constantia, Sheila has a decorator's eye for detail; the design of her beach house was inspired by wood panelling in an eighteenth-century French interior, which included a fireplace and a pair of wall cupboards. Whaledance's interior is

painted in subtly different greys and furnished with pieces acquired from local furniture sales. Keen to maintain the atmosphere of a vacation home, Sheila drew on her experience of living in Provence, and, in addition to the panelling and subtle use of colour, she has chosen to exclude fabrics from the decoration of the beach house. American shutters replace curtains, and the floorboards are of recycled old yellowwood, acquired from a demolished church in Humansdorp, near Port Elizabeth.

Over the last few years the demand for beach homes in this fabulous setting has been increasing. The property boom has already seen significant changes in Hout Bay and Camps Bay, further up the coast. Along with other exclusive properties, Whaledance changed hands recently, and the Boardmans have moved on. Amid anxieties about the environmental impact of too many new developments in an area of outstanding natural beauty, residents now fear an invasion of wealthy outsiders.

Top left: *The main bedroom, which is in the attic, has a wooden bed from Sheila's former antiques shop, Bygones Antiques & Summer House.*
Top right: *An oil painting by Wendy Anziska hangs in the dining-room.*
Bottom left: *The guardian angels were designed by Peter Knipe.*
Bottom right: *The master bathroom is also in the loft. The travertine-topped marble table was designed by Sheila.*

# Welsh Long House

## Berwyn Mountains
## Powys

WALES

In a photographic career spanning more than thirty years, Fritz von der Schulenburg has captured on film some of the most beautiful, inspirational and decorative interiors in the world. His personal taste, however, leads him to places that are simple, natural and unadorned. The Welsh Long House, overlooking the English Marches on the edge of the Berwyn Mountains, reflects Fritz's passion for wild and open landscapes.

Hidden in a fold of the hills high above a beautiful valley, the property is approached by a rutted track that winds upwards from the valley floor through scattered flocks of hill sheep, whose presence adds an extra hazard to the slow, precipitous ascent. Protected from the prevailing winds by a ring of closely planted trees, and flanked by a gentle stream that falls noisily down a ravine, the original Long House buildings consisted of a small two-storey cottage, a barn and a stable, all in a row, and

two small farm buildings across a muddy yard. An old brass bed in an upstairs room and a collection of mildewed Bibles and religious pamphlets, piled neatly on a windowsill, were the only reminders of the Welsh farmer who had once lived in the cottage and tended the hardy hill sheep.

Fritz was quick to recognize the potential of the property. While retaining many of the original features, he made radical improvements, installing bathrooms and other twenty-first-century luxuries. The existing kitchen, with its cast-iron fireplace, had a low, smoke-stained ceiling, which he removed, eliminating the second bedroom above it and opening up the kitchen to the rafters.

The three buildings that make up the Long House are linked by low, narrow doorways. The cottage leads into the former barn, now an open-plan living-room with a vast fireplace, its whitewashed walls exaggerating its rustic origins. A ladder staircase at the far end of the room leads

Opposite: *The house nestles between two hills, which echo to the bleating of hundreds of sheep.*
Above, left: *The entrance to the original farmhouse is still used as such, but the old bread oven no longer works and the hall has become a cloakroom.*
Above, top right: *The lead cut-out against a window pane is highlighted by a drift of snow.*
Above, bottom right: *Snowfall adds an exhilarating drama to the views from the house.*

Above, top left: *The hayloft is now a gallery bedroom.*
Above, top right: *A comfortable corner seat in the living-room is covered with Turkish kilim cushions.*
Above, bottom left and centre: *Bedlinen is stored in a Chinese red lacquer cupboard; across the room are a wood-burning stove and an African ladder.*
Above, bottom right: *Colourful ceramics adorn the long metal shelves in the kitchen.*
Opposite: *The double-height kitchen was created by removing the original ceiling and the bedroom above.*

up to the former hayloft, which has been transformed into Fritz's gallery bedroom, and a second narrow doorway opens into the stable, now a guest bedroom, and a former cow byre, now a spacious and unusual bathroom. The guest bedroom, which is open to the roof beams, echoes the structure of the kitchen, and the simple whitewashed walls retain the original metal stays.

Stable doors from each of the buildings open out on to the courtyard terrace. The former muddy yard has been paved over in York stone, on which a vast lump of granite stands sentinel. The view over the surrounding lush countryside seems to go on forever, while the immediate foreground falls away to the rushing river in the valley below.

The Welsh Long House is a wonderful place in which to laze in the summer and watch the buzzards wheeling on the thermals. It is, in the words of the poet Roger McGough, 'a jumping-off

place', where on clear nights the moon seems to shine more brightly than anywhere else on the planet, or where, in autumn or winter, you can watch the weather fronts coming in over the marches below, as the house is lashed by relentless rain and the hills run with water; it is a place where the chance of being cut off by a blizzard is more than a possibility.

Our lives change and so, in consequence, do the places we frequent. Fritz has recently moved on from his Welsh retreat to a 400-year-old farmhouse beside a lake in Austria, and he is applying his unique talent to the restoration of this new property with his customary energy and enthusiasm.

Opposite: *Behind the free-standing bathtub are the original stone troughs used for feeding cattle.*
Above, clockwise from top left: *A guest bedroom is housed in one of the outbuildings; the main guest bedroom has a wrought-iron bed draped with Irish horse blankets; the wrought-iron bed that belonged to the former owner has been painted and given a new lease of life with quilts from Chelsea Textiles; Fritz's studio, with its 'stairway to nowhere', is in another of the outbuildings.*

# Ali Riza's House

## Köyceğiz

**TURKEY**

Many people seeking to balance a busy city life with a tranquil environment in which to spend their leisure time are attracted to properties near water. For those disillusioned with overpopulated beach resorts, there is always the peace and comparative solitude of an inland lake to consider. Whether your home is a simple houseboat moored on the mirrored surface of the water or a rustic cottage on the shore, the calm waters of a lake generate a harmonious energy.

Lake Köyceğiz is situated just north of Dalyan in Turkey, its untrammelled waters feeding into the Mediterranean a few miles away. Named after the long netting traps that fishermen would have set across this narrow stretch of water at the southern end of the lake, the Dalyan River, redolent of centuries of history, is watched over by the brooding remains of Lycian tombs, while a series of canals cuts through the beds of giant reeds that lead down to the sea.

Turkey has a history of earthquakes, and Lake Köyceğiz is presumed to be the result of a massive shift in the earth's crust more than seven thousand years ago. Local folklore, however, prefers a more fanciful explanation of the lake's creation and its uniquely salty water. The tale lays the blame on a neighbouring monarch's lovelorn young son who, rejected by the beautiful daughter of the king who reigned in that region, decided to dig through the dunes that protected the low-lying area from the sea. Salt water quickly engulfed the land, drowning the princess and her court in the process. Today the sulphurous waters of Lake Köyceğiz are home to loggerhead turtles and a sanctuary for a wealth of wildlife, and this timeless backwater has acquired a rare ecological importance.

Sema Menteşeoğlu can trace her family back to the fourteenth century, when the Menteşe beys (provincial governors) traded with the crusader knights and were treated as independent minor

Opposite: *Every summer a flock of around forty hens, under the charge of Sema's pet rooster, scratches around the walled garden.*
Above: *The most inviting corner in the walled garden of the konak (mansion) is the raised wooden platform, in the dappled shade of a grove of olive trees.*

Above, left: *Sema painted the zinc-covered door panel, inspired by primitive art. The restored and repainted dowry chest belonged to her father's nanny.*
Above, top right: *Sema's studio still looks like the kitchen it used to be.*
Above, bottom right: *An open shelf in the kitchen holds glasses and crockery.*
Opposite: *Sema and her daughters painted a cupboard in a Palio pattern. The three-legged mulberry table was made by Sema, and the olives on the top shelf were picked on an island in the lake.*

princes, even when their lands were incorporated into the Ottoman Empire. Her family's fortunes fluctuated throughout the centuries until her great-grandfather, Ali Riza Pasha, opened chromium mines near Fethiye and became a wealthy local benefactor, founding the town of Köyceğiz at the head of the lake. Sema was born in Ali Riza's house and grew up on the estate; the lake played an important part in her childhood.

After an absence of thirty years, Sema returned to her ancestral village in 1992, by which time she had become a successful artist and the mother of two daughters. To her disappointment, the estate she remembered so fondly had become run down, and much of the land had been sold to villagers. The house itself, built by Ali Riza in 1878 in the grounds of his ancestors' ruined palace, had been neglected following the deaths of the last of the family retainers, and was in a sorry state.

Top left: *The ground-floor winter room has a nineteenth-century Anatolian kilim and a handwoven sheet from Muğla on the divan. On the mantelpiece are copper* hammam *bowls and Çanakkale ceramics.*
Top right and bottom left: *The hall serves as a study, with Ali Riza Pasha's panelled desk and chair. The tall sculpture is an unfinished work by Sema.*
Bottom right: *The iron bedstead in Sema's bedroom was her father's, and the black-and-white textured panel above the bed is one of her works.*

Restoration was slow and painstaking, and the house, which catches the lake breezes from all four sides, is now considerably altered from the one Ali Riza would have recognized. Modest in size and practical in design, the original property was built in a square, with a spacious hall and four rooms on each of the two floors. Sema judged the nineteenth-century comforts, which would have satisfied her great-grandfather's expectations, to be primitive and inadequate for a contemporary lifestyle. Indoor bathrooms were gradually built to replace the tiled *hammam* in the garden, and the kitchen, once housed in an outbuilding, is now within the house itself, next to the winter room. The stone outbuilding has been restored, reusing the original materials, and has taken on a new role as Sema's studio.

Shielded from what remains of the working estate by an old stone wall, Sema Menteşeoğlu's idyllic retreat is shaded by ancient olive trees, while the garden and surrounding land produce citrus

fruit, figs, olives, sesame, pine kernels and pomegranates. Local markets are full of seasonal delicacies, and the lake is celebrated for its grey mullet, eel and Köyceğiz fish roe, which is still preserved in time-honoured fashion and sealed with a layer of beeswax.

Despite the advances of tourism and progress in Turkey, the lake has changed little over the centuries. The villages and an occasional house are set back from its apparently deserted shoreline, and its very existence is concealed by the rock-strewn, wooded terrain and groves of bitter Turunç oranges.

*A simply furnished guest room. The copper ewers were collected from different parts of Anatolia: each region has its own distinctive shape. The picture of the house was painted by Sema when she was fourteen.*

# Quartermaine House

## La Colle-sur-Loup
## Alpes-Maritimes

FRANCE

For many years Carolyn Quartermaine was a frequent visitor to the South of France, either to pursue her work as a textile and interior designer, to source antiques for her clients, or to see friends. She had always been aware of the modern art gallery that had been transformed from a seventeenth-century woodmaker's house in La Colle-sur-Loup, a village near Saint-Paul-de-Vence. For several summers in succession, she had taken a room above a bar in the village, returning at regular intervals to the simple bedroom with its washbasin in the corner, and the key hidden under a pot of geraniums.

Carolyn was fascinated by the idea of a modern architectural space in an old French village associated with such artists as Matisse and Picasso, who had frequented it in the early twentieth century. She was more than a little preoccupied with the idea of owning the unique building, but

when the property suddenly came on to the market, the asking price proved to be much higher than her budget would allow.

No buyer was found at that time, and three years later, in January 2001, the house was put up for auction. Having convinced herself that she was not really interested, Carolyn nevertheless attended the sale, arriving after the bidding had begun. The bidding frenzy that ensued remains a blur to her, but she ended up as the new owner of the property – which since its closure as a gallery she had never properly visited – at a fraction of the original asking price. Armed with the keys to its iron-framed glass front door, she went to inspect her purchase, only to discover an interior that, after years of neglect, resembled a war zone. Undeterred, she had a vision of how the property would look once it had been restored.

Opposite, top: *The front door of Carolyn's contemporary home opens directly on to the narrow main street of the small village of La Colle-sur-Loup. Opposite, bottom, and above: A roof terrace on the first floor looks down on to a small, gravelled courtyard garden and a plunge pool. The terrace is often draped with lengths of Carolyn's fabric.*

Top left: *All sorts of things are hung from this metal coat rack to provide Carolyn with inspiration.*

Top right: *The simple kitchen is in a corner of the living area on the ground floor. The ceramic sink came from a flea market in Brussels.*

Bottom left: *Carolyn found this crystal candelabra and vintage purse at a local flea market.*

Bottom right: *A Gustavian daybed covered in honey-coloured vintage velvet stands at one end of the living-room, opposite the kitchen, with a 'tulip' table by Eero Saarinen and a lantern from Morocco.*

The gallery's earlier incarnation had been masterminded by the French designer Jacqueline Morabito, who still lives in the village and has become a close friend of Carolyn. It had been Jacqueline who had originally recognized the spatial potential of the seventeenth-century property, hollowing out the interior to leave four rectangular spaces with concrete floors and walls. It took Carolyn four years to restore the property to Jacqueline's inspired minimalist concept, since she had to juggle her work in London with the logistics of overseeing a team of French builders.

The house is built over three floors, its open-plan design providing essentially one room per floor. There is an enormous living-room and kitchen on the ground floor, with a guest room at the back opening out on to a tiny gravel courtyard garden, which is shaded by an ancient olive tree and has an azure plunge pool at its centre. The first floor consists of an open-plan bedroom and a

The ground-floor living-room contains an intriguing combination of period furniture and objects and modern classics.

bathroom with a concrete bath, the austere wall decorated with a hand-painted branch of cherry blossom. By removing the flat roof and replacing it with a more traditional pitched one, Carolyn created a further sleeping area at the top of the house. This area, which is flooded with natural light, was also designated her studio.

As misunderstandings with the builders occurred, windows were fitted and then promptly removed, and a pale-grey plaster floor laid at ground level was damaged by the man digging out the pool. Despairing that her home would never be free of builders and their mess, Carolyn put her energy into sourcing a kitchen sink in Brussels, vintage radiators from local scrapyards and single pieces of furniture from local *brocantes* (flea markets) and sales in Nice. The reality of doing up a vacation home often threatens the romantic dream, and at times Carolyn felt herself falling out of

Above, left: *Carolyn's mural of a Japanese cherry tree adds a feminine touch to this concrete bathroom.*
Above, top right: *Carolyn has hung her hand-printed linen cloths at the window of her own bedroom, on the top floor.*
Above, bottom right: *The mezzanine dressing area just below the bedroom has a whitewashed floor.*
Opposite: *An antique chaise draped in another of Carolyn's fabrics stands with a French gilt-framed mirror in a corner of the living-room.*

love with the house. Now, though, with all negative thoughts banished, she is able to enjoy the peace and solitude of her French home, which is free of builders at last. The building's stark minimalist space is softened by swathes of Carolyn's own fabrics, many of them designed in her top-floor studio.

During the first months after she moved into the house, Carolyn would regularly drive along the coast and stop off at the less frequented beaches to swim and sunbathe, returning home via the outdoor market in Nice, where she could pick up some fresh local produce and browse in antiques shops.

Friends who have stayed with Carolyn both in the South of France and at her home in London comment that one property echoes the other. Both are white and sparsely furnished, and both are used essentially as blank canvases against which she can show off her designs and collections.

# Duncan House

## Klein Karoo
## Western Cape

SOUTH AFRICA

Klein (Little) Karoo is referred to by the locals as 'the place of great dryness'. The smaller of the two Karoo regions (the other being Groot [Great] Karoo), it is situated in the Western Cape province of South Africa and stretches from Barrydale in the west to De Rust in the east. Squeezed between the Outeniqua Mountains, which are full of rock formations and cave paintings, and the Swartberg Mountains, Klein Karoo is separated by the Langeberg Mountains from the fertile valley of the Breede River and the Garden Route, an area known for its wine production and ostrich farming. Klein Karoo's architecture and town planning recall the days when this part of South Africa was a British colony.

In 2000 a nineteenth-century cottage on a mountain slope 6.5 kilometres (4 miles) from the R62, a back road linking the town of Barrydale with Oudtshoorn, attracted the attention of Paul Duncan, at the time editor of *House & Garden*, South Africa's most prestigious interiors magazine.

Once occupied by sheep and bats, and for years used as a windbreak by wandering springbok, the cottage was a rough place. Built in 1850, it had been the former shelter of *bywoners*, tenant farmers who eked out a living from the surrounding fields, kept cattle and lived in low-ceilinged rooms blackened by woodsmoke. The building would originally have had a thatched roof and sash windows. These were replaced in the 1930s, when the side gables were lowered, a tin roof succeeded the thatch, and the columns on the porch were constructed.

During his restoration of the building, Paul deliberately kept the thick walls and the original ceilings, made from local river reeds, which he washed and scrubbed to clean them of years of soot. He resurfaced the original dung floors, replaced the front door with one that he had found in another derelict farm nearby, and installed wooden shutters against the metal-framed windows. The property

Opposite: *This unassuming nineteenth-century whitewashed building was formerly used by springbok as a windbreak.*
Above, left: *The sunny stoep gives wonderful views of the Outeniqua Mountains.*
Above, top right: *In the summer, most of the cooking was done outdoors; most of the meals were picnics.*
Above, bottom right: *A kitchen dresser bought from a dealer in the Voortrekker Road stores a collection of oil lamps from the local co-op; given the lack of electricity in the house, the lamps were in regular use.*

had only five rooms, one of which was rapidly turned into a bathroom, and Paul set up a shower outside in the veld, with a nearby large rock serving as a soap dish. According to Paul, there is nothing quite like showering in the open air, under a vast sky studded with stars. Even in the winter, when the temperature dropped below freezing, he would be undeterred, standing naked under the hot water, with nobody for miles around, save a herd of Nguni cattle and a few ostriches.

Paul and his friends would spend the long summer weekends walking up into the *kloofs* (valleys) in the nearby Outeniqua Mountains, swimming in the clear, icy lakes, and generally 'hanging out' on the stoep, reading and relaxing. With the nearest neighbour a good 12 kilometres (7½ miles) away, they tended to invite each other over for long dinners. Since the house was so small – with only two bedrooms, a sitting-room, kitchen and bathroom – any guests needed to be good friends. The lack of electricity meant that evenings were lit with paraffin lamps, while the water was piped to the cottage in rudimentary fashion from a waterfall 4 kilometres (2½ miles) across the veld, stored in an outdoor tank and heated by gas. The interior of the former sheep pen was simply furnished and, under its tin roof, was blazing hot in summer and freezing in winter. The farming family would have cooked on an open fire, which Paul still used, although the addition of a gas cooker made life a little easier and a lot less smoky.

On beautiful evenings Paul would take his sleeping bag and dig himself a hole away from the cottage. In the glow of a dying fire he would settle down for the night and watch the panoply of stars in the sky above. He felt as though he were wrapped in a blanket of silence and tranquility, a silence that was at times unnerving, but was the best antidote to his cosseted urban lifestyle.

Below, left: *Books stacked horizontally in the bathroom defy the need for conventional shelving.*
Below, right: *The bedroom opens on to the stoep, so in summer Paul could sleep with the door open, never knowing which of the creatures that walked the veld at night might pay him a visit.*
Opposite: *The simple sitting-room is furnished with a table from Delos and a* bateau-lit *from Mexico, both standing on a swept bare-earth floor.*

# Ekensberg Villa

## Lake Mälaren

SWEDEN

Lars Sjoberg, an acclaimed connoisseur of Swedish furniture and architecture, has interpreted the growing popularity of rural weekend retreats in a manner that has earned him the nickname 'the second King of Sweden' among his friends and admirers. Sjoberg used to be a senior curator at the National Museum in Stockholm. His passion is for the Neo-classical Gustavian style of the late eighteenth century and, to date, his personal portfolio consists of six properties. The houses are all built in the same style, and all are in his native Sweden. All have been immaculately restored by Lars and his wife, Ursula, who is a curator of Stockholm's royal collections.

The most striking of Lars's Neo-classical retreats is the beautifully restored Ekensberg Villa. Completed in 1790, the three-storey Italianate building is a monument to the Neo-classical influence that swept Sweden in the wake of King Gustav III's return from Italy in 1784. It is set on a series of

Page 94: *The three-storey Italianate villa situated on the shores of Lake Mälaren was completed in 1790.*
Previous page: *A Neo-classical tall-case Swedish clock and an imposing bust furnish a flight of stone steps.*
Above: *Very little of the furniture is original to the house, but five of the dining-chairs are. A modern copy of an original from the 1790s, the chandelier is in the process of having its crystal drops attached.*

formal terraces above Lake Mälaren, which is one of Sweden's largest lakes and flows into the Baltic Sea at Stockholm. The villa was built for a local Swedish governor by an unknown architect influenced by Carl Harleman, the man credited with the biggest decorating job of the eighteenth century after Versailles: that of the 608-room Royal Palace in Stockholm. The Royal Palace was apparently the first and last palace on which Harleman worked, and it took him twenty-six years to complete.

Harleman also built, in the countryside around Stockholm, a series of manor houses in which he redefined the French rococo style, giving it a distinctly Swedish flavour. According to Lars, all the manor houses subsequently built in Sweden, including those in his own collection, were modelled on Harleman's design, in which the ornate and sometimes elaborate French rococo was made more functional, and any unnecessary decoration was omitted.

Its division during the twentieth century into apartments had deprived Ekensberg of its unique character, combining majesty and simplicity, and when Lars and Ursula came across the villa in 1976, the essence of its Neo-classical design lay hidden beneath a crude contemporary makeover.

Both scholars in the decorative arts, the couple share a passion for rescuing houses. Their restoration projects are motivated by the desire to re-create authentic and historically accurate interiors, correctly furnished and decorated. The finished houses are used not only for their own pleasure but also as sites for the architectural restoration workshops that Lars runs for Stockholm University.

Lars attributes the exacting way in which he approaches the restoration of his properties to the influence of his father, who taught woodwork and metalwork at the boarding school that his young

Top left: *The entrance hall is paved with limestone slabs; a plaster medallion on the wall depicts Carl Harleman, an influential Swedish architect.*
Top right: *A grey-painted sofa is upholstered in a copy of an eighteenth-century floral fabric, and the stove of the same period has garlanded tiles.*
Bottom left: *French Directoire wallpaper in the dining-room reflects the Neo-classical influences of the early nineteenth century.*
Bottom right: *The subject of the portrait is King Gustav III.*

Top left: *This chest of drawers is similar to one that Lars once produced for Ikea.*

Bottom left: *A clock, its face hidden by a door, stands on the tiled stove in the master bedroom.*

Right: *The bed has been placed opposite a tiled stove that is original to the house. The walls are linen canvas panels decorated with Gustavian flowers and ribbons.*

son attended outside Stockholm. Lars grew up observing the craftsman's patience and tenacity, coupled with his belief that anything could be repaired or made. Lars's greatest joy in the acquisition of his various houses has been to coax them gently back to their original glory.

During the past thirty years, when he could not find suitable materials to replace the originals, Lars has used his university connections and the talents of his students, calling on individuals to stucco a ceiling, mix plaster and apply it in traditional eighteenth-century fashion, and even, if necessary, repair and reassemble porcelain stoves and other equipment. Inappropriate wall coverings have been carefully stripped away to reveal painted canvas panels, and pieces of furniture have been gently scraped of paint until their true Gustavian colours come through.

During this slow journey of discovery Lars developed a range of traditional Swedish furniture, which he made available to the general public through Ikea stores and subsequently through Move Möbler in Sweden. Bringing Gustavian style to the masses has helped Lars to finance as well as to fulfil his restoration dream, and to share this extraordinary knowledge with students and the public alike.

*To the left of the canopied bed in the master bedroom is an eighteenth-century doll's house.*

# The Showman's Wagon

## Buckler's Hard
## Hampshire

ENGLAND

A steam enthusiast since the tender age of seven, Mary Montagu-Scott would go with her mother every year to the Netley Marsh steam rally near Southampton, where the local steam engines would gather for three days. Her mother's was a Burton wagon, built by Orton & Spooner around the turn of the twentieth century for a showman of the time, George Pickard, whose initials are engraved in the frosted-glass windows. Showmen owned and managed the touring fairgrounds and would travel the country in their custom-built wagons, setting up the rides and amusements at country fairs.

Mary's mother acquired the wagon in its original condition from train enthusiast Bill McAlpine in the 1970s, complete with bingo cards from fairground days and a pair of golden dancing shoes, which she found in the lockers. The paraffin lamps and the stove were still in good working order and, although the ceiling was black from years of coal fires, the interior was in fine condition.

On arrival at a fair, Mary would climb on to the wagon's roof to attach the chimney. A fire would be lit, and a kettle would be placed to boil, while fairground old-timers, some of whom remembered George Pickard's wagon, would get together and regale each other with stories of bygone times.

Mary, who is now an interior designer, has since become the owner of the showman's wagon, although in winter it is still stored in her mother's old barn. When the days start to lengthen, Mary's thoughts turn to bringing the wagon out of hibernation, brushing off the cobwebs and mice droppings, checking the tyres and towing it slowly to the family's home at Buckler's Hard, where it sits on the lawn, once again an object of beauty and curiosity. When it is not on the road, the wagon doubles as a spare room for guests, a playroom for the children and a refuge for Mary on busy days.

In scenes reminiscent of Mary's childhood, the first tasks on the wagon's arrival at Buckler's Hard are to set up the chimney, put down the wooden steps and reposition all the interior equipment, which has had to be dismantled and stored for the journey. The children are armed with dusters, and the spring-cleaning and polishing begin in earnest; the smell of beeswax fills the air. The fire is tested, and the first cup of tea of the year is made and then savoured on the steps. The cut-glass panels, the gold leaf and the mahogany are all gleaming. The children bring in posies of flowers from the garden, cushions and books appear, and Mary's special sanctuary is ready for another summer.

Every wagon was built to order, and no two are the same. Mary regards hers as a precious antique that requires endless care and attention. The exterior has to be meticulously repainted in deep gloss paints, rich as treacle, with a skill only to be found nowadays in the world of yachting. The paint is rubbed down between coats and gold leaf is applied to the ornately carved corners and

*Pages 100–101: For months on end, the wagon would stand in a beech wood near the home of Mary's mother, Belinda Montagu, on the edge of the New Forest. The peace of the woodland setting was in stark contrast to the noise and bustle of the fairs.*
*Below, left: The initials BM, for Belinda Montagu, are engraved on the back door of the wagon.*
*Below, right: Fitted into a recess in the wagon is the original Hostess stove with a mirror and mantelpiece above, hiding the chimney flue, which is channelled to the right to create a small airing-cupboard.*

gold lining as a finishing touch. While the exterior will continue to be maintained to protect it from the elements, Mary has decided to leave the original Victorian interior untouched and unrestored.

The family now spend their holidays in Turkey, where Mary and her husband have built a proper holiday home – not one on wheels – and where there is plenty of space for the children, as well as hot water and all the modern comforts, but the showman's wagon still holds a special place in Mary's heart. For her, it remains the most magical and luxurious escape from the pressures of everyday life. On long summer evenings, she will sit on the steps of the wagon with her husband, a glass of wine in hand, and watch the swallows catching flies in the fading light. In the gathering gloom, they light the paraffin lamps and set a fire in the brazier, and when the wind blows the wagon sways like a ship on the ocean. It is still the place where Mary feels truly happy and content.

*The bed across the back end of the wagon can be concealed during the day by three sliding doors made of cut-glass mirror; the recess and the ceiling retain their original floral decoration.*

# Bruce–Alvis Vega Apartment

## Jaipur · Rajasthan

INDIA

High on the list of priorities when considering the purchase of a vacation house is usually its proximity to home. For people who want to acquire only one additional property, rather than a whole portfolio, the choice for those based in Britain tends to be limited to Europe and the Canary Islands, while Americans gravitate towards the Caribbean and the coast of South America, the deserts of Arizona and the mountains of Utah. Flights have to be cheap and regular, often booked in bulk on the internet at the start of every year, when the diary is scoured and 'prime time' allocated before other commitments can intervene.

Liza Bruce, a British fashion designer, and her husband, Nicholas Alvis Vega, have chosen to break with tradition. On this occasion they have acquired a vacation home in Jaipur, Rajasthan's celebrated 'pink' city, a twelve-hour flight from London. The discovery of their Jaipur apartment was

the result of an impromptu decision to join friends on a trip to India, a country they had never previously visited, and which initially overwhelmed them, before they were entranced by the charm and spontaneity of the Indian people.

Acknowledging that India was an unlikely place for a vacation home in the European or American mould, the couple were prepared to look at properties available either to buy or to rent, but they were discouraged by the endless string of new bungalows in outlying suburbs, all the estate agents appeared willing to show them. When they had almost given up hope of finding somewhere with local historical character, they were led down a dusty alleyway in the bustling Muslim quarter at the heart of Jaipur to a beautiful, decayed mansion that had been built in 1880 by a British architect, Sir Samuel Swinton Jacob, for an official of the Maharaja's court. The Maharaja's descendants live

Opposite: *The apartment is situated on the top floor of a nineteenth-century mansion in Jaipur.*
Above: *Liza and Nicholas prefer to sleep in a red canvas tent on the roof. The red armchair is trimmed with cowrie shells.*

The walls of the study, which incorporates a library, are painted lime green, a treatment based on traditional Indian pigments.

there still, but an abandoned ten-room apartment at the top of the building, complete with a vast roof terrace with views over the city and the surrounding mountains, was available to rent. Rather than acting as a deterrent, the obvious decay and air of dereliction attracted Liza and Nicholas, an artistic duo who recognized that the abandoned rooms would encourage an imaginative interpretation of the generous space.

Unlike their Indian neighbours, whose interiors tend to be dark and sparsely furnished to counteract the oppressive daytime heat, Liza and Nicholas chose to reflect the life and colour of the city in the use of exotic and vibrant tones. The result is an exuberant kaleidoscope, with rooms painted hot pink, vibrant orange and lime green. Original stone floors are scattered with colourful rugs and pillows, and the walls have been painted by Nicholas with great swirls of pattern, inspired

by the embroidery seen on vintage saris. Silvered glass balls and mercury drops combine with lanterns in the shape of stars and, along with bowls of flowers and plants in pots, adorn many of the surfaces or are found suspended in clusters from the painted ceilings with other objects designed by Nicholas. The rooms are filled with the scent of fresh roses, marigolds and jasmine, an inexpensive luxury in India.

In such a hot climate a roof terrace is essential and provides a private place to relax. Liza and Nicholas have erected a large red tent on the roof, and it is there that they spend much of their time, eating and entertaining, often sharing meals with troupes of monkeys, who will make light work of leftovers on an abandoned plate. Tents play an important part in Indian life, and many of them are richly themed and decorated to imitate grand palaces. In addition to

*The colour of the hand-painted living-room walls was inspired by vintage saris. An Afghan susani covers the floor.*

entertaining on the roof terrace, Liza and Nicholas also use their tent as a bedroom, preferring to sleep outdoors.

Since restoring the apartment, the couple have been spending nearly six months of the year in India and continue to be a source of fascination to their Indian neighbours, who are still unaccustomed to having Europeans living in their midst. In return, the Indian culture and way of life have exerted their subtle influence on Liza and Nicholas, and they have fallen under the country's spell.

Opposite: *At the entrance to the apartment, the fanlight above the door is picked out with a hand-painted leaf design.*
Above, left: *One of the guest bedrooms has a door that opens on to the study.*
Above, top right: *Access to the mansion building is through a grand double-height entrance hall.*
Above, bottom right: *The kitchen is hand-painted a deep purple.*

# Davidson House

## Calvados

### FRANCE

Typified by its *maisons à colombage*, or black-and-white timber-framed houses, Calvados – a *département* of Normandy on the north-west coast of France – is recognized today as much for its beautiful rolling countryside and apple orchards as it is for the long, sandy beaches that will forever be associated with the Normandy landings of 1944.

In reference to a trend established nearly two hundred years ago, when the fishing villages of Normandy began to attract artists, writers and poets, who in time were followed by the fashionable crowd from Paris, Normandy is jokingly referred to today as the 21st *arrondissement* of Paris. Thousands of Parisians have chosen to buy or rent weekend cottages and holiday homes there. They have been joined by a large number of Britons, attracted by Normandy's proximity to the south coast of England and by the easy journey across the Channel, as well as by the region's celebrated gastronomy.

Anglo-French designers John and Monique Davidson work from London but part-own a seventeenth-century timbered manor house in a remote Normandy hamlet, to which they and their two daughters retreat whenever they can. Owned by Monique's relatives for many years, the property passed out of the family's hands for a while, leaving Monique and her sister, Michele, feeling bereft and strangely displaced. When the house came back on to the market in the late 1980s, the sisters and their husbands decided to buy it back. Fortunately, in the intervening years few changes had been made to the original interior. The sisters have kept the beamed ceilings, the old tiled floors and the original, untouched wallpaper. Following the house's return to the family, the interior was treated to a fresh coat of paint, and the kitchen – the most important room in the house – was modernized. Only essential maintenance has been carried out since.

Opposite, left and top right: *The black-and-white half-timbered house represents a distinctive architectural style in Calvados.*
Opposite, bottom right: *A rustic wooden coat rack in the entrance hall bears testimony to the mixed weather in the region: sou'westers and rubber boots for the winter; straw hats for the summer.*
Above: *A rustic praying-chair stands beside the telephone table in the hall, at the bottom of the simple wooden staircase.*

The house is long and low, with windows on either side and fireplaces in every room. Its decoration and simple, relaxed furnishings respect both its age and its origins, and it has been filled with antiques and pieces found at local *brocantes* (flea markets) in Caen, the regional capital, founded by William the Conqueror. The rooms resonate with the memories of a lifetime of travelling, and include collections of much-loved and unusual objects, works of art and spontaneous purchases.

The pace of life in the region is slow, with the locals apparently taking the time to savour every minute, especially on market days. The nearest town to the Davidsons' house is Saint-Pierre-sur-Dives, which is a hive of activity every Monday, when it hosts the largest market in Calvados. Local produce on sale at the market includes butter, thick fresh cream, the famous Camembert and other cheeses, lobster, seafood and saltwater fish; there is lamb from the salt meadows near Mont-Saint-Michel, as well as the cider and calvados, or apple brandy, for which the region is renowned.

With outlets in Japan and the United States, as well as in Europe, the Davidsons do a great deal of travelling and have little time to themselves. Their tranquil retreat in Calvados gives them rare moments of relaxation with friends and family, but these days, a weekend break is often combined with work trips to Paris. At the Monday market in Saint-Pierre-sur-Dives the couple catch up on local news while filling their baskets with fresh produce. Afternoons may be spent taking long walks along the beaches of Cabourg, a town of impressive seaside architecture, made famous by the writer Marcel Proust. Alternatively, there is the nineteenth-century seaside town of Houlgate, where an assortment of beautiful villas and chateaux overlooks a fine sandy beach, which offers the possibility of a stroll after a lunch of *moules frites* at Les Vapeurs in Trouville.

Below, left: *Stacks of unbound antique books adorn a Biedermeier desk.*
Below, right: *An armchair in a corner of the sitting-room has covers made of J. & M. Davidson ticking.*
Opposite: *Also covered in the Davidsons' ticking, the large cushions on this wrought-iron cot make a good contrast with the black-and-white tiled floor.*

# Watts–Gurney House

### Byron Bay
### New South Wales

AUSTRALIA

Byron Bay is located on the north coast of New South Wales, two hours' drive south of Brisbane and its famous Gold Coast. An important location on the 'hippie trail' in the 1960s and 1970s, the small town retains a bohemian image. In the intervening years, the hippies have been replaced by surfers, artists and intellectuals, all attracted by the sense that 'anything goes' in Byron Bay. The town overlooks a beach of clear, white sand and crystal water offering world-class surfing. Expert surfers tend to go to the beach beyond the iconic lighthouse, which stands on a hill above the town, where the waves are bigger; the beach on the other side of the point, called Broken Heads, is less frequented and in some ways more beautiful.

Miv Watts spent the early years of her life in London, but after the death of her husband, Peter, she and her two children travelled to Australia, where she worked in films and television, designing

and styling costumes and sets. She enjoyed the enthusiasm and easy-going style of her Australian friends, and had the pleasure of watching her children grow up in a country where anything seemed possible. During the eleven years she spent in Australia, Miv never visited Byron Bay, and it was not until 2001, when she returned to the country on vacation, that she and her partner, Mike Gurney, visited and fell in love with the place – and promptly bought a house there.

Miv and Mike found their house after making an offer on a different property in Byron Bay. They were in Sydney when they heard that the initial deal had fallen through. To overcome their disappointment, Mike made Miv get in a car and drive with him back to Byron Bay – a journey of eight hours – to view the only house that they had not previously visited on the list drawn up by the local estate agent.

Opposite: *The property is set back from the ocean, surrounded by a protective planting of mature trees.*
Above, top left: *Miv and Mike often swim in the natural pool near the house.*
Above, top right: *The simple house has a corrugated-iron roof.*
Above, bottom left: *The couple spend much of their time relaxing on the antique sofa on the verandah.*
Above, bottom right: *The doors opening on to the terrace from the main bedroom are always open.*

The property was almost perfect. Although it was set back a little further from the ocean than they would have liked, Mike and Miv were captivated by the sense of tranquility pervading the place, as well as by its abundant wildlife. The building, which has a simple corrugated-iron roof, was constructed in the 1980s by a master craftsman using salvaged materials dating from the Federation period of the early twentieth century. The couple bought it without a moment's hesitation. They now exchange the often bleak winters in Norfolk, England, where Mike runs a successful fishmonger's and Miv an interior design consultancy, for blissful Australian summers.

When they stay at their house in Byron Bay, Mike and Miv spend most of their time on the verandah. They keep windows and doors open day and night, adapting their living habits to those of the Australian wildlife with which they are now obliged to share their home. Guests can expect to

Opposite: *All meals are eaten outdoors on the porch, which is decked with colourful lanterns at night.*
Above, left: *The cool hallway, with its polished wooden floor, is decorated with wooden tracery.*
Above, top right: *The sitting-room is furnished with an Indian sofa and coffee table and an assortment of colourful, textured cushions.*
Above, bottom right: *The kitchen is painted in subtler shades of the two colours that Miv used to decorate her kitchen in Norfolk, England.*

Above: *This bedroom's walls have been painted a shade of green that harmonizes with the vibrantly coloured textile on the bed. The bedhead is made up of a Japanese coat.*

Opposite: *Doors from the sitting-room open on to a bedroom on the left and the porch on the right.*

be woken in the early hours by the sound of kookaburras cackling in the nearby eucalyptus trees, accompanied by the heavy thudding of possums enjoying a wrestling match in the roof space above their beds. Other distractions include green tree frogs and a python that has taken a liking to the shed. Koalas are occasionally sighted in the gum trees surrounding the property.

If the house appears to be idyllic, so too are its immediate surroundings, which include ancient volcanic mountains, dense rainforests and tumbling waterfalls, while the land in front of the property falls away to the ocean. Miv and Mike have found plenty of reasons to feel extremely happy with their new vacation home.

# Dunton Hot Springs

## Colorado

USA

A former Colorado mining village that housed the region's first European settlers in the late nineteenth century, Dunton Hot Springs is set in a mountain valley at the end of a dirt road leading south from Lizard Head Pass, about 48 kilometres (30 miles) south-east of Telluride.

Typical of the mining settlements of its day, the village is made up of weathered log cabins with rusty tin roofs, and, at first glance, appears unchanged from the day in 1944 when the Emma Mine's seam of gold dried up. Closer inspection reveals, however, that far from being a ghost town, Dunton has been reinvented. The old cabins have been restored and brought up to date, with mended windowpanes, modern plumbing, electricity and telephones, beds with fine blankets and artefacts from around the world adorning the walls. One of the cabins even boasts a bath in the floor, fed by a natural hot spring.

The project is the accomplishment of a dream long held by European partners Bernt Kuhlmann and Christoph Henkel. Influenced by John Wayne movies and Zane Grey novels, they were enamoured of Western American culture, and when they discovered Dunton it was as if they had stumbled into one of their childhood fantasies. They recognized that Dunton gave them an opportunity not only to preserve a historic piece of the Wild West but also to share a unique and idyllic getaway with other like-minded people. They bought the ghost town in 1994. At the time Bernt was quoted as saying that the culture of the American West was probably the most popular with children of all ages around the world, simply because it is a culture of escapism. People who live in cities from London to Tokyo are now buying into the dream, and paying for the privilege of immersing themselves in the nostalgia of a bygone era.

*What was once a remote ghost town in the Colorado Rockies has been transformed into an exclusive resort. In the film* Butch Cassidy and the Sundance Kid, *it was the place where the outlaws went into hiding after robbing a bank in Telluride.*

Above, top left: *This original cabin is one of the eleven restored buildings that make up the village.*
Above, right: *The hottest of the hot springs is protected by a large teepee.*
Above, bottom left: *An original sign has been incorporated into the restored bar and meeting-room.*
Opposite: *Guests can while away the long winter evenings in the well-stocked library.*

Where existing cabins were too dilapidated to be restored, other original cabins were found in the outlying mountain valleys and transported by truck or by helicopter to Dunton, where they were restored and added to those originally found in the village. The result is a unique retreat of eleven rustic nineteenth-century guest cabins and other buildings, restored by local craftsmen, overshadowed by the awesome peaks of El Diente and Mount Wilson in the San Juan Mountains, and combining the rugged feel of the Wild West with the service and quality one would expect to find in a six-star resort.

The original 'saloon' has been enlarged and converted to house a bar, meeting-room, dining area and lounge. The bar is scarred with the initials of Dunton's long-departed miners, and the lounge smells of polish and is furnished with tasteful antiques and rugs. Today the log cabins look

much as they must have done at the turn of the twentieth century, with bearskin rugs and Navajo artefacts; wood-burning fires and underfloor heating, together with an endless supply of piping-hot water, have been installed to satisfy the twenty-first century's insistence on comfort.

For those buying into the dream, Dunton has a wealth of possibilities. In the summer, with the desert and a vast Native American reservation on its doorstep, it offers trips on horseback or mountain bike to Monument Valley, the Canyon of the Ancients and the Valley of the Gods. During the winter months, when the settlement can be cut off from the outside world by snowdrifts, guests can go heli-skiing on the 4300-metre (14,000-foot) peaks that surround the resort, or explore the immediate area on snowmobiles or in snowshoes, ending the day relaxing in a hot spring under the stars or in the refurbished bathhouse. The combination of water naturally

Opposite: *The bathhouse, which has been perfectly restored, contains one of Dunton's three hot springs.* Above: *Many of the cabins have been restored as authentic period bedrooms; this room includes antique snowshoes and a Navajo rug.*

Above, top: *This guest cabin has its own hot spring. The large tin tub holds cold water for cooling off.* Above, bottom, and opposite: *The bedrooms are furnished with bearskin rugs and elk-hide bedspreads, and decorated with Navajo and other tribal artefacts.*

heated to a temperature of 41°C (106°F), exercise and altitude can make for an almost out-of-body experience.

This special place is affordable only to a few, and Dunton's inaccessibility and remoteness, which lie at the heart of its appeal and exclusivity, ensure its protection from mass tourism. It offers a retreat for those who live permanently in the glare of the media spotlight, as well as for those who just need to get away from it all for a while.

## Tounis

### La Castellane
### Tarn-et-Garonne

FRANCE

English-born interior designer Kathryn Ireland has achieved a good work/life balance. She is based in Los Angeles, where she has a thriving decorating business, but the prospect of her three sons growing up there without experiencing a different culture prompted her to look for a bolt-hole in Europe. It seemed inevitable that she would gravitate back to Britain to choose a second home, but two wet weeks in Somerset proved so discouraging that the family moved on to France without a backwards glance.

In the late 1980s many English people were buying houses in the Dordogne or the Lot, but despite some hard searching, Kathryn failed to find the right property in either area. The family started exploring the Tarn region and was soon introduced to Tounis, a working farm with chickens in the kitchen, geese in the yard and a French family spanning at least three generations looking after the place. Kathryn fell in love with the farm and its setting, in the rolling hills between Montauban and

Pages 128–29: *Tounis has an idyllic setting, and in spring its façade is draped in purple wisteria.*

Above, top left: *Lunch is usually eaten at about 3 pm in the huge barn, which has its own working kitchen.*

Above, top right: *An enormous open fireplace is the focal point of this cosy sitting-room.*

Above, bottom left: *Examples of 'work in progress' can be seen in Kathryn's light-filled study.*

Above, bottom right: *Local farm prints hang on the wall behind a pair of chairs in loose covers made from chenille bedspreads.*

Albi, and bought the property that same afternoon. It was only later that she discovered that in mid-April Tounis is transformed by a mass of lilac blossoms blooming in the hedgerows.

The house itself – a rabbit-warren of rooms, subdivided by endless partitions – would have been a challenge for any designer. It had six bedrooms but only one bathroom, on the ground floor. Kathryn began by retiling the roof and then opened up all the rooms, returning them to their original, high-ceilinged proportions; the large central hallway on the ground floor opened into rooms on either side, an arrangement characteristic of many Quercy farmhouses.

Kathryn's sons are now in their teens, and she contrives to spend between three and four months every year with them in France. It is their home, perhaps more than anywhere else, and the thought of moving – a possibility that has been discussed, if only tentatively – fills all three with horror.

With the property restored and the adjacent eighteenth-century *pigeonnier* renovated by her brother, Robert, for use as guest accommodation, Tounis can sleep up to twenty people; with Kathryn's love of spontaneous entertaining, there is often a full house. While in France, Kathryn keeps in touch with her demanding clients in Los Angeles by telephone and email; the long, restorative days are otherwise spent horse-riding, biking, reading, eating and catching up with friends. Typical teenagers, the boys now sleep until lunchtime, so their day does not start until Kathryn's is partly over.

The wine produced from the vineyards on Kathryn's 20-hectare (50-acre) estate is managed by the former owners of the farmhouse, who moved into a smaller property nearby and produce a handsome 10,000 litres (2200 gallons) of *vin de table*. Kathryn's table is always well provided for; the rest is sold through the local co-operative.

*The large, beamed kitchen, converted from a cow barn, is dominated by a locally made table.*

Local markets in Montauban and Gaillac provide endless diversion for guests, and Kathryn spends time trawling through the local *brocantes* (flea markets) and small antiques shops in the area, looking for furniture, which she reupholsters in her studio at the farm and ships back to California. Such is her reputation after so many years in the area that many dealers now seek her out, driving over to Tounis with van-loads of furniture for her to inspect in anticipation of a major sale.

Tounis has given Kathryn and her family the chance to experience what she likes to think of as 'real living'. She collects milk from a neighbouring farm at the end of her drive; she has planted an organic vegetable garden and, as an enthusiastic and consummate cook, enjoys creating delicious meals while having the opportunity to catch up properly with friends and family.

Opposite: *The rustic bathroom is situated in the restored* pigeonnier, *which was built in 1750 and is now used as a separate three-bedroomed house for Kathryn's guests.*
Above: *The blue-and-white pictorial fabric used in the first-floor guest room came from Paris.*

# Overwood

## near Haworth
## West Yorkshire

ENGLAND

Artist Celia Lyttelton now lives all year round in a seventeenth-century weaver's cottage on the Yorkshire moors. The cottage used to be her retreat from London, and the place to which she would disappear to paint, but it was reduced to a burnt-out shell in the late 1990s. What remained of the fire-blackened stone walls of the listed building has been rebuilt, and the exterior has been restored to exactly the way it was on the day that Celia and her father found the cottage by chance while out walking.

Overwood is situated in a wooded valley on the edge of a steep hill, surrounded by rivers and waterfalls. Beyond lie the moors immortalized in Emily Brontë's novel *Wuthering Heights*, where the wind howls over a wild and beautiful landscape. Three months after her discovery of the cottage, Celia was presented by her new landlord with an antiquated lease, which allowed her to hunt fowl

on the land and to have builders for only one month to help her make the property more habitable. The house had neither running water nor electricity. Since the only access was along a vertiginous dirt track, building materials had to be wheeled in by barrow. While the fireplaces were rebuilt Celia and Andrew, her husband at the time, camped out at the cottage, huddled up to gas heaters to ward off the February cold.

Once the month was up and the builders had moved out, Celia set herself the task of clearing the remaining rooms in the cottage and the outlying barn of all the years of accumulated junk, from enticing hippie literature of the 1970s to old pressure cookers; there were even ancient Ministry of Defence food cans, the remains of Second World War rations. The work took Celia a year, at the end of which the barn had been transformed into her etching studio.

Enjoying the restoration of the cottage, Celia resisted her husband's inclination to look into traditional plastering methods and left most of the existing plaster intact on the old walls, covering it with a mixture of watered-down UniBond and water-based varnish. The furnishings were acquired piece by piece, or were discovered amid the debris of generations of workers, and a few textiles and paintings were given by friends who came to stay at the cottage to paint. Never particularly liking the ethos of the 'weekend cottage', Celia has always preferred her friends to come and go as they please, staying days, weeks or sometimes months, free to interpret the property as they wish.

A water system was cleverly rigged up by the builders during their month of occupation, and the water was heated by a contraption almost identical to the one at the Brontë Parsonage Museum down the road. Until a gas booster was installed, washing-up was done in cold water and often

*Page 134: Celia's studio is through the arch at the near end of the seventeenth-century cottage.*
*Previous page: The large windows provided the weavers with sufficient light for their work.*
*Below, left: Celia's studio has been set up in the barn.*
*Below, right: The narrow trestle table and bentwood chairs were found amid the junk left by previous inhabitants of the house. The walls were painted with raw pigment and varnish. The painting of a pheasant is by Melissa Scott-Miller.*

in the dark. During the winter months, friends who were brave enough to leave the comfort of their centrally heated London flats and wend their way north would often remain the entire day in bed, surrounded by hot-water bottles, while Celia would collect and chop wood to feed the four fires, and climb under the waterfall to clear the water pipe, which regularly silted up. Evenings were spent by candlelight, a romantic necessity that was probably the cause of the fire that eventually destroyed the cottage.

Out of the ashes, Celia has built a replica of the seventeenth-century cottage, and from the outside there is nothing to suggest that it is not the same as it used to be. Friends who continue to visit have noticed a marked improvement in the facilities, however. The cottage now has not only running water but also electricity, although the atmosphere is very much the same as it ever was.

*A large daybed has been placed under the window in the entrance hall of the cottage.*

# Beach House

## Shela · Lamu

**KENYA**

Lamu is a seductive island in the Indian Ocean, located two degrees below the equator. A narrow channel separates it from mainland Kenya, and planes land on a rough airstrip on neighbouring Manda Island. Fleets of small boats line up at the wooden jetty to ferry new arrivals through the mangroves to Shela, the resort end of Lamu, famous for its miles of sandy beaches.

Lamu Old Town, Kenya's oldest town, gives visitors an impression of stepping back in time, enhanced by the use of donkeys rather than cars in the narrow streets and alleys. In its long history, it has been a thriving port, trading with the Arabs in the sixteenth century before its discovery by the Portuguese. Arab dhows with crescent-shaped sails were used to export mangrove timber, ivory, amber, spices and slaves. By the mid-nineteenth century Lamu had come under the rule of the Sultanate of Zanzibar, which controlled Kenya's coastline until the country's independence in 1963.

*Page 138: Evening meals are served on a simple wooden table beneath a massive baobab tree in the secluded garden, where a myriad twinkling ships' lanterns provide illumination.*
*Previous page: The central courtyard of the villa is dominated by a swimming pool with views over the beach and the stretch of water that separates Lamu from Manda Island.*

Lamu has become a popular retreat, not only for those living in Kenya seeking a few days at the beach, but also for many tourists from further afield, who are drawn to the island to relax, meditate and rediscover themselves. Time is of no importance there; the hands of the clock barely seem to record the hours.

While Shela has seen significant development in the past ten years, few people are fortunate enough to own a property on Lamu, and houses for rent are in constant demand. Built in the dunes on the edge of Shela's shoreline, Beach House faces the Indian Ocean, its concrete and coral-stone façade bathed each morning in the warm glow of the rising sun. The villa's thick walls are plastered with lime and it has a thatched *makuti* roof, traditional to the region, beneath which is a shady terrace with views over the beach.

Instead of the traditional courtyard, Beach House has at its centre a 'horizon' swimming pool, one side of which faces out to sea. The house is furnished in typical Swahili style, with benches and tables made by cabinetmakers in Lamu using eighteenth-century pattern books. Persian rugs, which have been shipped to Lamu for more than four centuries, have been placed on top of the local grass matting.

The designers and owners of Beach House – the most prestigious of four properties available to rent – have designed it for vacationers who love the simple beach life and appreciate hot showers, a lack of clutter and, above all, privacy. The house is surrounded by a garden full of tropical plants, and the open-plan living-room looks out over a tiled dining terrace, flanked by imposing acacia and baobab trees. On the terrace, meals can be enjoyed in shade by day or by the light of dozens of

Opposite, top and bottom left: *Guests often while away the hottest time of day on the roof terrace, beneath the traditional thatched* makuti *roof.*
Opposite, bottom right: *Another spot for a siesta is the comfortable, cool sitting-room beside the pool.*
Above: *The house has a spectacular location, right on the beach at Shela, the resort end of Lamu.*

Above, left: *The bathroom is simple and comfortable.*
Above, right: *Each bedroom is dominated by a swathe of mosquito netting. In this room, a row of striped kikois adorns the wall beyond the low bed.*
Opposite, top left: *Beach House's castellated terraces give views of the public beach.*
Opposite, top right: *A traditional bed in the shaded garden makes a good place for reading.*
Opposite, bottom: *A dhow idles in the shallows while an evening picnic awaits guests on the beach.*

storm lanterns at night. Five airy bedrooms, all furnished with local stringed daybeds and voluminous white mosquito nets, give views of the sea. Hammocks are slung from the heavy beams of the roof terrace; there, as the evening breeze blows gently through the thatch, visitors can lie and watch the fishing dhows coming into harbour for the night, their silver nets glinting in the moonlight.

Beach House offers the ultimate in luxury beach vacations: a tastefully decorated villa, complete with its own chef, set at a discreet distance from neighbouring properties on the outskirts of Shela, with an unimpeded view of one of the most beautiful stretches of coastline in the world. It is small wonder that families make a habit of returning there, making believe that for a couple of weeks a year this island paradise belongs to them.

# Los Piños

## Majorca

SPAIN

Standing in the main living-room at Los Piños, gazing out over the balcony to the azure sea below, you could be forgiven for believing this house to be an ocean-going liner, afloat on the mesmerizing waves that pound the rocky coastline of this exclusive promontory of Majorca.

The room combines brilliant-white walls, constantly reflecting the different moods of sun and shadow, with a variegated blue-tiled floor. The open-plan, split-level space emulates the effect of the peaks and troughs of waves in a heavy swell, and leads out through a vast picture window on to a balcony that is as wide as the house. The extraordinary illusion of being afloat is increased by the continuation of the maritime theme: collections of model boats, old brass telescopes, a sextant and a ship's barometer are displayed, and one wall is covered in a collage of stuffed fish in glass cases, hooks and fishing tackle.

This unique vacation home was designed and built for his family by Paco Muñoz, a renowned Spanish interior designer. Starting in 1964, he took three years to circumnavigate the problems posed by the rigidity of his design and the house's location, balanced precariously on the granite rocks at the water's edge. Paco made the job even more difficult for himself by refusing to remove any of the trees or plants on the site, insisting instead on building around these natural obstacles. He bought several old winches from the port of Bilbao to help install the huge windows with their tall shutters, and extra equipment was also required to erect the mast, which he acquired from an old boat and positioned below the swimming pool, and from which flutter the Spanish and French flags.

The house has three levels, which are set back from one another. The lowest is the sea itself, where there is a small jetty and a flight of steps cut into the rock rising up to the second level, on which

Opposite: *Appearing almost to grow out of the rocks on which it sits, Los Piños is built in an austere style. Its bare concrete walls are softened only by the continuous curves of the design and the unhindered encroachment of nature.*
Above, left and top right: *The swimming-pool terrace, a little way down the cliff, is tiled in blue.*
Above, bottom right: *Orange trees are one of the distinctive features of the inner courtyard.*

are the swimming pool and secondary bedrooms. From there, steps outside and a circular, tiled stair inside lead up to the top level, which houses the living-room, master bedroom and guest rooms.

Influenced by Arab architecture in his design, Paco included as many windows and patios as possible. The windows, which are kept open throughout the summer, slide into the walls and are positioned to take full advantage of the prevailing sea breezes and the house's south-facing aspect.

Filling the house is the sweet smell of orange blossom from a small inner courtyard connecting the living-room with the principal bedrooms, while cypress trees and purple bougainvillea are framed by the numerous windows, like paintings against the blank backdrop of the textured walls. There are no pictures or ornaments, save the many objects that claim an obvious association with the sea. Paco relies on the varied textures in his design and on the property's natural surroundings for decoration.

*The living-room is open on all sides and offers spectacular views over the Mediterranean. It is furnished with comfort in mind, and the wooden bamboo-style frames of the sofas and armchairs were designed by Paco himself.*

The maritime theme continues in the leeward approach to the house, where a heavy front door, like the louvred cupboards in many of the rooms, is made of solid teak. Taken from the cabins of an old tea clipper, the wood has been polished until it shines, and the handles and fittings are fashioned from antique brass. Much of the furniture was designed by Paco specifically for the property, reflecting an obsession with maintaining a particular theme in each of the houses he has modelled over the years.

In the forty years since Paco Muñoz's inspirational design, Majorca has developed into a popular international holiday destination. Its rocky coastline, picturesque harbours and hilltop villages have been subjected to a building and restoration boom that has transformed the island, but many of the new properties lack the panache of Paco's groundbreaking 1960s development.

Opposite: *An outdoor staircase descends from the open-plan living-room to the swimming-pool terrace.*
Above, left: *Paco designed all the furniture in the house, from the simplest wicker basket to the unique structure of the master bed.*
Above, top right: *The master bedroom includes a comfortable area for sitting and relaxing.*
Above, bottom right: *A louvred shutter connects the open-plan living-room to nature beyond the glassless window.*

# Château
# de Moissac

## Moissac-Bellevue
## Var

### FRANCE

Lying between Nice and Aix-en-Provence is Var, an area of France well known for its wine, olive trees and truffles. The village of Aups boasts the largest truffle market in the region. Neighbouring Moissac-Bellevue is an unremarkable village amid this rural idyll, but when Louis and Marie-Christine Cavaglione discovered the abandoned seventeenth-century chateau on Moissac's outskirts, they realized that it was their joint destiny to restore it to the ultimate fantasy. Overwhelmed by the size of the property, the immensity of the rooms and the height of the ceilings, and daunted by its decrepit state, the Cavagliones nevertheless recognized its potential as the perfect restoration project, and it has been their consuming passion ever since.

The last seigneur of the chateau had been obliged to relinquish his home in unseemly haste in the face of the citizens' uprising at the time of the French Revolution, and the property

Page 150: *Evening sunlight softens the austerity of the simple entrance to the* bastide.

Previous page: *The graceful sweep of the stone staircase in the stone-flagged entrance hall, lit by an antique crystal chandelier, leads up to the* piano nobile.

Above, clockwise from top left: *No vegetation obscures the façade of the* bastide; *a massive nineteenth-century cupboard fits in the kitchen as if it had been designed for the space; a row of metal chairs lines one wall of the* piano nobile.

endured various changes of ownership over the centuries before being abandoned completely. The restoration of the fabric of the building has taken ten years – ten years in which Louis Cavaglione researched the provenance of the stone, copied existing floor tiles and faithfully replicated each of the elements unique to the building's construction. At the same time he incorporated such twenty-first-century comforts as underfloor heating. The bathrooms, although equipped with old baths and porcelain washbasins, have been fitted with modern taps and plumbing.

As the interior was restored, Marie-Christine trawled the antiques shops and flea markets of Nice and L'Isle-sur-la-Sorgue looking for pieces to fit the scale of the chateau. This proved to be very difficult, since most things looked so small in rooms of such vast proportions. She began by

choosing the chandeliers, which are mainly antique crystal and wonderfully heavy, and then found the massive kitchen cupboards, which were almost an exact fit.

The emptiness of the rooms reminded Marie-Christine of her Italian origins, of the palazzos in Sicily and, in particular, of Donnafugata, the beautiful country home of Don Fabrizio, prince of Salina, in Luchino Visconti's celebrated film *The Leopard*. Inspired by the atmosphere created in the movie, she was determined to preserve the extraordinary sense of space in the chateau and to make a statement by using only one or two special pieces of furniture in each of the rooms, rather than crowding them.

The monumental fireplaces and the soft grey of the limewashed walls lend the seventeenth-century chateau a contemporary air. Marie-Christine has enhanced this by adding an enormous sofa

Top left: *The* piano nobile *is empty but for a row of expectant mismatched chairs.*
Right: *Shafts of light fall on to the floor of hexagonal terracotta tiles in one of the many sparsely furnished rooms. The tiles continue through the doorway into the dining-room (top), with its exquisite chandelier.*
Bottom left: *The architectural beauty of the* bastide *is reflected in the simplicity of its many rooms.*

*An Italian baroque bed with a painted headboard
graces one corner of a vast, high-ceilinged bedroom.*

in one room, a baroque bed in another, and an informal row of metal chairs in the *piano nobile*. The pieces she buys are inevitably rare and expensive, and sometimes months go by in which she finds nothing suitable. She has put up mirrors in the rooms that are still waiting for furniture, so that they are not completely empty.

When they are not travelling, Marie-Christine and Louis spend the working week at their home in Nice and drive out most weekends to Moissac. A wide terrace, with views over the surrounding fields of peacefully grazing sheep, is used all year round for al fresco dining and for lounging in the sun. Winters in the region can be mild, with a soft, mellow light and clear, invigorating air. If the weather does break, family and friends retreat to the kitchen, which is dominated by an enormous fireplace and a long wooden table.

The restoration of an old property is never complete, and Marie-Christine helps finance the project by renting out the chateau as a location. Its grey, textured walls and period details in the echoing reception rooms make an ideal backdrop, especially for a wedding.

The most memorable event to have taken place at the property recently is the wedding reception of the Cavagliones' only daughter. Following a simple marriage ceremony in the village chapel, the wedding party progressed back through the meadows below the chateau, where Marie-Christine had set out tables decked in white fabric, each with a garland of olive branches and dominated by a huge candelabra. Dinner followed in the main salon of the chateau, and the guests danced through the night beneath the twinkling lights of the antique crystal chandelier in the entrance hall. For the Cavagliones, the occasion was a fitting tribute to the creation of their family fantasy.

Left: *Even though the bathrooms are modern and have underfloor heating, they still preserve a sense of the building's antiquity.*
Right: *A frothy black evening dress by Scherrer of Paris lies abandoned beside the bed before the massive eighteenth-century fireplace, which has been painted to resemble stone.*

# Hecktermann Cottage

## Suffolk

ENGLAND

Not every cherished rural retreat resembles a stereotypical picture-book cottage with tendrils of scented honeysuckle around the door. More often than not, such houses are unaffordable and unavailable, and found in places that are already too popular to merit the term 'retreat'. So it was that when Kirsten Hecktermann was looking for a holiday home in Suffolk, she rejected the idea of a pinkwashed, beamed cottage typical of that part of the country, and opted instead for a pre-war concrete prefab that had been delivered on the back of a lorry and assembled in three weeks. Originally intended as temporary accommodation for farm workers returning from the war, the unprepossessing shack had withstood the test of time and was still standing more than sixty years later, with barely a repair to its original construction.

During the Cold War, the land around the cottage had been turned into an army range, and for

forty years the surrounding grassland, which is now mown and sold as turf, was closed to the public. As a result, the area had not been intensely farmed and was home to a rich wildlife, and the nearby coastline had been saved from the caravan parks and estates of bijou bungalows that mar parts of Britain's seaside today.

Dwarfed by a massive concrete farm building, which was its immediate neighbour, Kirsten's cottage was situated on the edge of a farmyard. Although its position precluded the luxury of a garden, the lack of private outdoor space was more than made up for by the proximity of beautiful, unspoilt countryside, miles of coastal walks, secluded picnic spots and beaches from which to swim.

Kirsten chose her prefab as a place where she could be alone: a simple environment providing basic creature comforts but no luxuries, not even curtains. A fireplace in the sitting-room was the

Opposite: *Most of the furniture and bits and pieces were bought cheaply as job lots at local auctions.*
Above, top left: *Space is at a premium, and Kirsten has had to devise clever storage solutions.*
Above, top right: *The exterior of the prefab, although largely unprepossessing, is given a certain charm by the plants that scramble over the roof.*
Above, bottom left: *Coats and hats are kept in the narrow entrance hall beside the staircase.*
Above, bottom right: *The house is surrounded by wildlife-rich countryside.*

only source of heat; when the temperature dropped below freezing, Kirsten surrounded herself with hot-water bottles and wrapped herself in antique quilts to keep warm.

The unexpected resilience of the prefab recently prompted the farmer on whose yard it has stood for so many years to smarten up his farm and make more use of the outbuildings. It was time for Kirsten to move on, but she wanted to stay in Suffolk. This time she chose a pinkwashed, beamed cottage, and, together with her partner, spent a summer clearing the garden of nettles, collecting fallen apples and starting to address the endless problems that come with the purchase of a 500-year-old building.

*The interior of the cabin is furnished with random old pieces, including daybeds and sofas bought from local markets and auctions, their sagging springs and dated covers disguised under lengths of antique fabric and piles of hand-embroidered cushions, which are Kirsten's stock-in-trade.*

# La Casa de la Palmera

## Gaucin · Andalucía

SPAIN

Gaucin is perched on the steep hillside of the Sierra del Hacho between Gibraltar and the town of Ronda. Developed by the Arabs, it was built around the Castillo del Aguila on the remains of a Roman fort; its rocky foundations gave rise to the name Sagra Guazan ('strong rock'). Today it is one of the most beautiful villages in the highlands around Ronda; its predominantly Moorish architecture and streets of whitewashed houses are typical of the *pueblos blancos* ('white towns') of the region, and straddle the steep hillside in terraces around the ruins of the old castle.

The village has appealed to travellers, painters and sculptors since the nineteenth century, and continues to attract a similar mixture of creative people of various nationalities, who have bought and restored houses in the village. Among them are Brenda Hartill, an artist, and Harold Moores, a classical record specialist and gardener, who were introduced to Gaucin one winter in the 1980s by

their friend Val Jauncey, who owns the Blackheath Gallery in London. The weather in London was particularly miserable that winter, and the couple had been talking for a while about the idea of buying somewhere in the sun. Optimistic about what they might find in Spain, before leaving, they had started to investigate the possibilities of borrowing money to finance a purchase.

On their first morning in Gaucin, Brenda and Harold had breakfast on the terrace of Val's house, with a fading crescent moon still visible over the church and the castle in silhouette above it, and fell in love with the village. They recognized that its great charm lay in its strong connection to the land and the fact that many of the houses had been built by local families, whose descendants continued to live in them. Conveniently, the village bank manager doubled as the estate agent; he took them to see several available properties, including La Casa de la Palmera. Captivated by the old and semi-ruined courtyard house, which was dominated by a huge palm tree and far larger than any property they had considered for a vacation home, the couple promptly put in an offer and bought it within a week.

The house was characterized by eccentric changes of level, reflecting the variations in the massive rocks on which it stands, but although the roof was slightly raised, the structure of the property had been left largely undisturbed. Brenda and Harold were anxious to retain as much as possible of the original fabric, preserving paving and tiles as well as the crumbling outer courtyard, the walls of which were apparently held together by vines and bougainvillea as old as the house. The village team employed to do the building work mixed the cement by hand, and their handiwork helped to maintain the property's quirky angles and crooked walls. Restoring houses, particularly abroad, is often an expensive and hazardous business, and many new owners embark on such a

*Pages 160–61: The garden terrace, which includes an eighteenth-century wellhead, is furnished with benches, cushions and a table, and has views over the village to El Hacho mountain.*
*Below, left: The courtyard contains a large palm tree, after which the house is named.*
*Below, right: In the Moorish cottage, an open-tread staircase leads to the gallery bedroom.*

project with the intention of renting out the house to repay the investment. With the help of her architect friend Mark Potter, Brenda set out to restore the courtyard house, determined to retain its authenticity and unique ambience, but in such a way that it would offer as much flexibility as possible to the rental market. The result is four self-contained apartments, which can be let whenever the family is away from Gaucin.

Instead of being encumbered with fake beams and poured-concrete floors, Palmera has been restored with love and attention to local detail. The front door – complete with bayonet gashes from the Napoleonic Wars, when Gaucin was a strategic fortress on the mountain pass to Gibraltar – was rescued from a nearby house. So successful has the restoration been that the couple are loath to leave Gaucin and often find themselves staying in the house even when they have paying guests.

*The entire ground floor is covered with local handmade terracotta tiles, and the walls have been decorated by hand. Most of the shutters, doors and pieces of painted furniture were found in the local market at Sabinillas.*

# Conran House

## near Bordeaux
## Gironde

FRANCE

Jasper Conran saw his house in the farming country east of Bordeaux as a retreat from his frantic life in London. As one of Britain's leading fashion designers, with a career spanning twenty years, Jasper is regarded as an authority on British style and is credited as the designer who does 'English with an edge'. In addition to a successful fashion label, he also designs crystal, china and cutlery for Waterford Wedgwood and an exclusive range of clothes for Debenhams department stores. It was not surprising, therefore, that he needed a house away from the bustle of London where he could be tranquil, garden in his potager and entertain his friends.

Jasper bought the house years ago as a virtual ruin for a mere £5000, having spotted it on a walk while staying with a friend in the region. It had been abandoned ten years previously, and time, weather and bats had wreaked havoc on the fragile roof. Essentially just a shell, the house was

without electricity and running water, and the garden was little more than an overgrown field with two lime trees, which Jasper kept and which continued to shade the house in summer. Jasper remembers it as being 'a beautiful mess' but, although he replaced the roof almost immediately, he did nothing else to the house for a while, preferring to travel and explore the world before settling down.

With some of his wanderlust satisfied, Jasper returned to France and began to restore the house in earnest, installing the utilities, replacing windows, repairing and renewing shutters, and searching for old terracotta tiles to match those already on the floor, which was mostly earth. The house's simple design made it surprisingly cosy, and in summer Jasper laid striped antique dhurries on the floors amid a general scheme of his favourite blue and white. Using paint, he created an interior that combined cream, beige and green, complemented by unlined cream curtains.

*Opposite: Badly neglected for more than a decade, the garden was gradually brought under control.*
*Above, left: The potager yields an abundance of produce throughout the summer.*
*Above, top right: Terracotta pots line up in front of a window, its frame painted blue to match the shutters.*
*Above, bottom right: A solitary spot for rest and relaxation offers wonderful views of the surrounding farmland.*

Most of the furniture was found in junk shops, reflecting Jasper's unerring eye for beauty and functionality and his ability to spot a bargain. The curtains were made of old linen sheets, and the sparse but comfortable furniture was inexpensively reupholstered in similar fashion. In the winter, replacement sets of curtains dyed in more suitable dark tones of red, blue and green complemented the thick wool carpets that usurped the summer dhurries.

Jasper believes that a house symbolizes the lives of its occupants and should never be static. He is conscious that an interior does not simply come together overnight but needs to be considered carefully and developed by stages. And so it was that in France, away from the pressures of work, he was content to spend his time cooking and pottering about in the garden as the property slowly evolved.

Opposite: *Everything in the house bears witness to Jasper's eye for functional beauty: in the sitting-room, an enormous sofa with acid-green and yellow cushions offset by a bold blue-and-white-striped rug doubles as a spare bed.*
Above, left: *A sofa upholstered in midnight blue flanks a refectory table in front of a wood-burning stove in the kitchen.*
Above, right: *The table and bowl in the corridor were designed and made by a friend, Eric Pearce.*

Left: *Each of the bedrooms is furnished with a bateau-lit; the linen and quilts were sourced locally.*
Top right: *The curved end of the bateau-lit adds elegance to the guest room.*
Bottom right: *Jasper discovered the capacious armoire in a local junk shop.*

Although passionate about gardening, Jasper had never thought that he could make a garden in France until he planted some garlic and watched it grow. It was only a few years before an impressive 3 hectares (7 acres) of kitchen garden was created. Herb beds, lilies, old-fashioned roses and an orchard of fruit trees followed, and the garden became a personal sanctuary encircled by poppy-sprinkled wheat fields.

The house in France became the place to which Jasper preferred to invite his friends for a weekend or a few days, as he could properly enjoy their company there rather than being obliged to squeeze them unsatisfactorily into his busy London schedule. While they enjoyed his hospitality, and relaxed and luxuriated in the effortless simplicity of his home, Jasper would be working away at his vegetable patch or planning a new addition to the garden, loving the idea of 'playing house'.

Since the sale of the French house, Jasper's friends have been privileged to enjoy a more English style of hospitality at his 500-year-old timber-framed country house in Suffolk, where he manages to spend most weekends when he is in Britain. Who knows where his predilection for playing house will take him next?

Left: *A free-standing tub with elaborate vintage taps dominates the simple bathroom.*
Top right: *The blue-and-white-striped cotton dhurrie on the floor enlivens an otherwise pale colour scheme in this beautifully cool bedroom.*
Bottom right: *The mahogany* bateau-lit *in the guest room has been paired with one of Jasper's huge signature sofas.*

# Tangala

## Zambezi

ZAMBIA

Some 15 kilometres (9 miles) upstream of Victoria Falls, on private land facing the setting sun, Tangala stands on a large, sweeping bend of the Zambezi River, just inside Zambia. Virtually invisible from the river, where crocodiles and hippos lounge and grunt, the house is located on the riverbank against a backdrop of tall ebony trees. The long, single-storey, terracotta-painted building has a roof of grass thatch and was completed in 2000 for Ben and Vanessa Parker and their three children.

In the late 1980s Ben bought a plot of land in the area with a friend, William Ruck Keene, and they designed and built a lodge, called Tongabezi, which they ran as a business. Later, Ben and Vanessa met and married. By the time two of their three children had been born, the rondavel at the Tongabezi camp had become too small for the family, so they decided to build a new home, Tangala,

a short distance upstream. Ben now commutes from their new home to Tongabezi by canoe; on the journey home in the evening, he regularly runs the gauntlet of an inquisitive hippo.

Work finally began on the foundations of Tangala nearly six years after Ben had first approached the landowner, Mr Mufalali, to purchase the site on which it stands. Building a new house in Africa on the scale the Parkers had in mind is not a challenge every family would be prepared to accept. In addition to the political uncertainties inherent in any project on that continent, the logistics of building a house in a spot so far from civilization, and all the problems associated with getting materials and workers to the site, required patience and expertise. The Parkers called in Giles and Bella Gibbs, interior designers who have a special affinity for and love of Africa, and whose work on their own home in France the Parkers had admired.

Opposite: *Seen in a hippo's-eye view, the house is nearly invisible behind the trees on the banks of the Zambezi River in Zambia.*

Above: *The circular terrace originally planned under the thatched roof was enlarged to improve the proportions of the room.*

The ambitious project had not advanced very far when Giles and Bella arrived in Zambia, expecting the structure of the building to be in place. With more than seventy people on site, most of them unskilled, there was a great deal to organize. The only people who seemed to know what they were doing were two local carpenters and a Zimbabwean plumber known as the Doctor of Pipe. The original plans for the house had been drawn up by a South African architect, Fred Spencer. Giles and Bella spent the first few weeks making constructive changes to the design, tempering the slightly austere look of the planned exterior and suggesting ideas for the interior, including furniture and soft furnishings, much of which had to be made specially for the property. They also suggested enlarging the windows, tripling the dimensions of the circular terrace and eliminating the buttresses intended for the exterior wall.

Opposite: *The large kitchen is dominated by a long refectory table with 1940s Shaker-style chairs; an entire wall holds shelves for storage.*
Above, top left: *The 'snuggery' adjoins the sitting-room. Shelves have been ingeniously fitted under the stairs.*
Above, top centre and right, and bottom right: *Pointed arches emphasize the height of the ceilings.*
Above, bottom left: *A shady outdoor room has cushions made of West African mud cloth.*

*This glamorous bathroom provides exhilarating views of the garden.*

Progress was slow. With no electricity, the house had to be constructed using only mechanical tools, and building was further complicated by the fact that Giles was obliged to work with a spirit level that had no fluid and a tape measure with the numbers worn away. For three months the rough track to the main road was flooded and impassable, and, while bricks were made on the riverbank, the thatch for the roof, together with all the other materials, had to come by river. Supplies would often be months late, if they turned up at all.

It was to take a full year for Tangala to come together. The finished house mixes Islamic, African and Mediterranean elements with the Gibbses' European sense of colour and use of textiles, and furniture and fabrics bought in South Africa. It is now a fully functioning family home for nine months of the year. The Parkers' three children go to school in Victoria Falls, crossing the border into

Zimbabwe every day, a practice that necessitates a very early start for everyone. During the school holidays the house is generally let. The family spend Christmas in Britain and Easter in South Africa, and they often go to Minorca in August for big clan gatherings.

Tangala's location on the river near a national park means that there have occasionally been uninvited guests, from a herd of sixty elephants, who decided to take up residence one year and munch their way through much of the Parkers' woodland, to individual hippos grazing on the lawn, a temptation for the family's two dogs, who like nothing better than to chase the local visitors off the premises.

Top left and bottom right: *The various bedrooms are cool, comfortable, shady spaces, and many have connecting bathrooms.*
Top right: *A guest bedroom has an interesting metal frame for the mosquito netting above the bed.*
Bottom left: *Gum poles made locally by Kubu Crafts support a bed canopy in the main bedroom.*

# La Herrumbrossa

## Tarifa · Costa del Luz

SPAIN

Arvid Bergvall spent his childhood holidays in Marbella, southern Spain, where his parents had a vacation home. As they grew up, Arvid and his friends would head to the coast in the heat of August to take advantage of the unbroken 10-kilometre (6-mile) stretch of white sandy beach at Tarifa, located between Cadiz and Algeciras on the Costa del Luz ('coast of light'), the closest point in Spain to North Africa. Some years later, Arvid spent his honeymoon there; he and his wife, Beth, later bought a building in the old fishing town.

Forty years ago, Tarifa was virtually unknown and unacknowledged by the swarms of surfers who now congregate there every summer to 'catch' the waves and hang out in the local bars and hotels. When my family took vacations there, the descent to the beach led us through lines of eucalyptus trees and gnarled olive groves before we reached the sand dunes that in those days

protected this part of the Spanish coast. All three children learned to swim in the surf, strapped to cork buoys 'borrowed' from fishermen's nets, to make sure that they were brought back to safety on the next big wave. The beach was always deserted. There was no one to disturb the tranquility and isolation except for the Guardia Civil, who patrolled the shoreline at midday looking for illegal boats and abandoned contraband from Africa. In more recent years Tarifa has become a national park, its beautiful coastline protected from property developers yet topographically changed by the army of wind turbines that now punctuates the skyline, taking advantage of the winds from Africa.

From their home in the old town, Arvid and his wife eventually gravitated to the coast, drawing on his growing interest in architecture and interior design to develop and build their own vacation home, barely 200 metres (650 feet) from the beach. Created from five existing ruined buildings,

*The collection of low whitewashed buildings with roofs of traditional pantiles is located close to one of the most beautiful beaches in Spain. The architectural simplicity is enhanced by the terrace, which overlooks the ocean and is hung with billowing white curtains.*

La Herrumbrossa is a substantial property that sympathetically combines traditional architecture with a modern, uncluttered interior. The couple set about making one home, retaining as many of the original architectural features as possible, such as roof shapes, thick walls and alcoves. To help finance their beach existence, they went on to build another villa and a guest house on the site, both of which they rent out on long-term contracts, and plans are in place to build more houses over the next three years.

Since they were living on a beach, the couple decided to create a simple, contemporary interior, where the sand brought in by their two little daughters would be easily swept from the pale limestone floors. To ensure that their house, unlike many vacation homes in Spain, could be enjoyed all year round, they installed fireplaces and wood-burning stoves to keep them warm in winter.

Opposite: *The living-room is comfortably if sparsely furnished, and has an open fireplace for winter. The photograph beside the fireplace is by Alexis de Vilar.*
Top: *Built-in banquettes double as spare beds in the study, which has a wood-burning stove.*
Above: *The spacious kitchen has wooden units handcrafted by carpenters in Tarifa. The large window overlooks the terrace, and the room connects with the dining-room, furnished from Timeless, a Marbella-based interiors store.*

Above, top left: *The main bedroom has been kept deliberately simple. The photograph on the wall beyond the bed was a present.*

Above, bottom left and right: *These two contemporary bathrooms were designed by Arvid Bergvall.*

Opposite: *In the main bedroom, a standard lamp made from a sculptural piece of driftwood has been placed next to a photograph by Alexis de Vilar, purchased at an exhibition in Barcelona.*

The couple spend more than eight months every year in Spain, and intend their children to have a local education while they are young enough to adapt easily to Spanish culture and learn the language. The children are encouraged to appreciate the beautiful natural surroundings during the time they spend at Tarifa, and they would appear to enjoy a blissful existence.

While Arvid takes advantage of the onshore breezes to windsurf and try his luck at kitesurfing, Beth and the children build sandcastles and swim in the sea. All of them enjoy walking in the hills behind the house and exploring the shoreline, where cowrie shells were once ten a penny. Whales and dolphins are also drawn to this exceptional stretch of coast, and orcas have been sighted in spring. Once a week the local farmer brings his herd of goats down to La Herrumbrossa to graze. Childhood memories are made of this!

# Tizac

## Gaillac · Tarn

FRANCE

The Tarn is a relatively little-known region of France, named after one of the country's longest rivers, which rises in the Cévennes mountains and flows for more than 320 kilometres (200 miles) to join another mighty river, the Garonne, before emptying into the Atlantic Ocean. Frontier country for most of its history, this region of the Midi-Pyrénées, with its citadels and fortified villages, offered the kind of unrenovated property that photographer Tim Beddow and his wife, Sophia, were actively seeking as a retreat from London.

Along with others before them, the couple had scoured Provence, the Côte d'Azur, the Dordogne and the Pyrenees, dismissing each in turn for various reasons: overcommercialization, overcrowding, a surfeit of English people, or simply an unreliable climate. Their quest, which they had thought would be a reasonably easy one, was to find an authentic property in an unspoilt part

of France with more hours of sunshine than they would find in England, a second home in need of restoration and at an affordable price.

Heading north and away from the Mediterranean, the couple stopped at Gaillac. There they knew an estate agent with a good knowledge of the Tarn, an area dotted with working farms and medieval fortified villages, and encompassing countryside in which vineyards marched with oak woods where wild boar and deer sought refuge from hunters.

When they came to the end of a particular gravel track, the couple knew that their search was over. Ignored by many, the nineteenth-century farmhouse that greeted them was in a dilapidated state, having been neglected and unlived in for more than fifteen years. The windows and front door were crooked, the plasterwork of the façade was crumbling away from the mud-brick structure, and broken pantiles lay where they had fallen from the roof. Typical of buildings in the region, the property consisted of a two-storey house with a barn attached in which hay would have been stored and livestock housed. The erstwhile occupants would have lived a relatively simple existence on the ground floor of the house, cooking on an old range in the vast fireplace. Bedrooms were wooden cubicles built into the corners of the main room. A primitive stone sink was the only apparent means of washing; all other bathroom activities took place outside. Water was drawn from a nearby well 40 metres (130 feet) deep, and that was the limit of available utilities; electricity was an undreamed-of luxury.

The timeless character of the property and its position on the edge of a wood worked their magic on Tim and Sophia. They tracked down the elderly owners to their modern bungalow not far away and discovered that they were only too delighted to be rid of the old house, Tizac. A few days

*Pages 182–83: The timeless character of the property and its position on a gentle slope on the edge of a forest were instant attractions. The dark-blue wooden shutters go well with the pink limewashed walls. The main terrace, outside the kitchen, is where nearly all lunches and dinners are consumed.*
Below: *The main room of the barn combines kitchen and sitting area and extends to the terrace; the red sitting-room is in the farmhouse. The door leads through to the barn.*
Opposite: *A primitive bark painting from Bali hangs in the barn next to an English dresser and a* table vigneronne, *on which stands a wire-mesh* garde manger *from a local flea market.*

Left: *A desk and chair take up one corner of the red sitting-room, which is linked to the barn.*
Top right: *The walls of the red sitting-room are painted with coloured limewash, and the original glass in the windows has been replaced.*
Bottom right: *The main bathroom has a large dark armoire and an Indian chair from Goa.*

later, with a deposit paid, Tim and Sophia returned to London the proud owners of what they referred to thereafter as their 'French wreck'.

As the couple discovered, the majority of properties in the area were constructed in response to prevailing weather conditions. Thus walls that would bear the brunt of summer storms were built of stone, while the more sheltered sides were made of mud brick and plaster, to save money. The couple's first winter at Tizac was spent rebuilding the less robust walls, and insulating and retiling the roof of the barn.

Tim and Sophia were agreed that the secret of the property's appeal was its simplicity. Tim was convinced that they could restore the building themselves, without involving an architect or an interior designer. The two of them needed little encouragement to abandon London and spend six

months in the Tarn. They decided that the wonderful square barn, with its original wooden framework, would be made into the main living-room, opening on to a large terrace. They installed a kitchen along the length of one side, and added windows with views over the woods. At the far end of the room they built a massive open fireplace, around which a sitting area of comfortable chairs and a sofa has been created. The adjoining farmhouse has become guest accommodation.

Occasionally, during the restoration process, as the property came to resemble a battlefield rather than a comfortable home, the couple would look at each other and question their sanity and judgement. Fifteen years on, now that other newcomers are moving to this once undiscovered region of France, they realize that this was probably the best decision they have ever made. Tizac is a constant pleasure, an oasis in which they can take refuge from the real world whenever the mood takes them.

*The main bedroom has an Indian rattan chaise and an Egyptian screen at the end of the bed. The painting was bought in India and represents a Himalayan mountain scene.*

# Tou Dao Gou

## Miyun County

CHINA

In 2002 Juan van Wassenhove, a Belgian financier working in Beijing, was fortunate enough to take over the lease of a weekend cottage in Tou Dao Gou, China, from a journalist working for *Time* magazine who was returning to Rome.

Tou Dao Gou is a hamlet of no more than 250 people situated at least three hours' drive from the centre of Beijing in the far north-eastern corner of Miyun County, near the border with Hebei Province. Much of the county's boundary is defined by China's Great Wall, including the Simatai section and the Gubeikou Pass, one of the key north–south corridors through the Yan Shan mountains.

One compensation for Juan's long commute to his weekend hideaway is the pleasure of having the Great Wall of China as a backdrop to the cottage. The Wall was begun more than two thousand

years ago by Qin Shi Huangdi, the first emperor during the Qin dynasty (221–206 BC). Shi Huangdi conscripted peasants and anyone not working the land to connect and extend four ancient fortification walls, and stationed armies as a first line of defence against the invading nomadic Hsiung-nu tribes north of China. One of the largest building projects ever, the Great Wall stretches across the mountains of northern China, winding north and north-west of Beijing.

Qi Jiguang, a Chinese general during the Ming dynasty (1368–1644), was the man responsible for the sections of the Great Wall that Juan and his friends climb at weekends and that he can glimpse through the windows of his cottage. In charge of rebuilding, defending and maintaining an 800-kilometre (500-mile) section of the Great Wall, Qi Jiguang was an innovator, using fired bricks and stone slabs instead of roughly hewn rock to construct the wall.

Opposite: *The communal garden is planted with flowers, fruit, vegetables and spices, while corn hangs to dry from the slate-tiled roof.*
Above, left and top right: *The Great Wall, which serves as a boundary between Hebei Province and Miyun County, is clearly visible from the cottage.*
Above, bottom right: *A neighbour's cottage can be seen through the open doors of the dining-room.*

*The space between the bedrooms doubles as a pantry and dining area. The concrete walls are covered in plastic wallpaper, with the lower part painted blue; this theme of blue and white is extended to the painted wooden furniture and doors.*

During the brief autumn, when the weather is good – a time the Chinese describe as *tiangao gishuang*, meaning 'the sky is high and the air is fresh' – Juan explores the crenellated parapets near the cottage; although seriously eroded over the centuries, they still bear the mark of the kiln where the bricks were fired. Their continued existence is testimony to the high standards that Qi Jiguang brought to his work, and which earned him the reputation of being the most feared and, at the same time, the most respected individual of his day. Beijing was not invaded during his watch.

Juan's cottage in Tou Dao Gou, owned by the head of the village, is part of a small commune of similar buildings. Formerly a peasant's living quarters, the cottage is made up of four small rooms forming the northern side of a courtyard, with a separate kitchen building along the eastern wall. Juan has turned three of the rooms into bedrooms; the fourth combines a living area, dining

area and pantry. The rest of the plot is occupied by a patio and a fertile garden, and beyond the courtyard gate is a communal outhouse. Although by no means elaborate, the cottage is clean and comfortable, and its monastic simplicity provides a welcome refuge from the pressures of work in Beijing.

As Chinese and foreign investment in Beijing continues to grow at an alarming rate, the city authorities are looking for new areas in which to build housing. The village leader, Juan's landlord, has been approached by property developers from the municipality seeking to invest in a hotel and golf course. For the moment, scarcity of water in the region has halted the project, but it will not remain that way for long. Proper roads are starting to encroach on this rural outpost, and with them will arrive the hordes of Beijing's growing middle class, looking for weekend retreats of their own.

Left: *The overhead light in the master bedroom is a red wooden ornament inscribed with Chinese characters denoting wealth, prosperity and happiness.*
Top right: *The floral fabric used in both bedrooms was bought at the village market.*
Bottom right: *Saucers are decorated with images of Mao Zedong at different stages of his career.*

# Plettenberg Bay House

## Western Cape

SOUTH AFRICA

Plettenberg Bay, on the famous Garden Route that follows the coast of the Cape, the southern tip of Africa, is renowned for its miles of empty white beaches, its tranquil lagoon and the spectacular backdrop of the Outeniqua and Tsitsikamma mountains, with the rugged and forested Robberg Peninsula at its furthest point. Unsurprisingly, this beautiful coastline has proved a popular vacation spot with South Africans and foreigners alike, and plenty of new houses have been built there.

One architect who has to his credit more than thirty properties along the Garden Route is Menno Meinesz, locally renowned for his talent at interpreting what his clients want from a vacation. Among those properties is this whitewashed vacation home overlooking the beach and the Indian Ocean. Its owners, who work in Johannesburg, decided on a house on the coast as the antithesis of their hectic city life, and commissioned Menno to create a thatch-roofed rondavel, characteristic

of the older houses around the Cape. This original brief did not pass the initial design stage, since the requirement placed on the architect to house the owners, their four adult children and their respective families made such an old-fashioned design impractical.

Instead Menno chose to design the new house around the owners' lifestyle, which required an easy-going, adaptable living space. The most challenging aspect of the task was that the couple wanted to spend time at the house on their own without feeling that they were rattling around in it, but when the extended family was assembled, the property needed to be able to accommodate up to ten adults comfortably.

The house occupies an area barely the size of a tennis court. Menno designed a central core consisting of a bedroom and study located above the main living-room, with a kitchen and dining

Pages 192–93: *A low wall encircles the whitewashed property. Wooden steps lead to the beach.*
Opposite: *The simplicity of the whitewashed living-room is enhanced by the bright textiles used in the soft furnishings and the vibrant blue-and-white colour scheme.*
Above: *The entrance courtyard works well as an al fresco dining area, with Lloyd Loom chairs painted in bright primary colours and a rusted Mexican candle sconce on the wall.*

Top left: *The study continues the blue-and-white theme, with an ottoman covered in a paisley throw adding an extra touch of colour.*

Top right: *Built-in shelves at the top of the spiral staircase are excellent for display. The wrought-iron candelabra was made locally.*

Bottom left: *A painted wooden Indian cow's head hangs on the wall in the dining area.*

Bottom right: *The main living area has a fireplace at one end and a dining area up steps at the other.*

area, all connected by a circular staircase. The result is a self-contained unit, perfect for two. An additional four bedrooms and living area have been created around the property's central well. Each of the guest bedrooms has a separate outside entrance, so the comings and goings of the junior members of the family do not disturb the others. Patios and terraces surrounding the house provide ample suntraps where individuals can spend time alone.

Displaying the talents of local artisans and craftspeople, the interior of the property is simple but enlivened by bright decorative detail. The entrance courtyard doubles as an al fresco dining area that is large enough to accommodate the entire family. Lloyd Loom chairs in bold primary colours set the tone for the general decoration of the house, which draws on a scheme of blue and white, appropriate to the proximity of the sea.

The Plettenberg Bay house does not pretend to be anything more than it is. Distinctive for its simple, Mediterranean-style architecture, the property is surrounded by a neat whitewashed wall that separates it from its neighbours. A set of rickety wooden steps leads down to the beach immediately below the house, from which dolphins and whales are regularly sighted. It continues to be a vacation home that is enjoyed by the family and their friends throughout the year, and a place to which they return to recapture a quality of life they have found nowhere else.

Left: *A guest bedroom has a moulded, built-in headboard painted watermelon pink. Each of the guest rooms has a separate outside entrance, so that other people in the house are not disturbed.*
Top right: *A custom-made wrought-iron four-poster bed is hung with Indian cotton saris.*
Bottom right: *Models of 1920s-style Swedish bathing beauties frolic on the wall of a terrace overlooking the beach.*

# Simplicity

## Mustique

ST VINCENT AND THE GRENADINES

Toronto-based architect Jack Diamond had long been in search of a holiday home where he could bodysurf in interesting surroundings, but he had studiously avoided the Caribbean island of Mustique, convinced that its reputation as a haven for the jet-set meant that he needed to look further afield for a surrogate for his native South Africa.

In 1987, however, encouraged by the recommendations of two friends – his attorney in Toronto and international designer John Stefanidis – Jack half-heartedly responded to an advertisement in the *Financial Times* for a property on Mustique. Unfortunately, the description of the property had wildly exaggerated its assets: the house was awful. Jack found, however, that, despite the initial disappointment, he was drawn to Mustique. The island's exclusivity and its limited number of houses meant that it was certainly not cheap, but the atmosphere was informal, the people were friendly

and kind, the natural environment was wonderfully unspoilt (unlike most other Caribbean islands), and it was away from the glare of the public eye.

Jack returned with his family to Mustique the following Christmas and met some of the celebrities who had found a refuge on the island. The visit gave him the opportunity to explore at his leisure the pre-volcanic atoll, which measures little more than 6 × 1.5 kilometres (4 × 1 miles). On the undeveloped side of the island, generally avoided on account of its winds and rough seas, Diamond found a plot of land next to a conservation area and protected from the open sea by a promontory.

It was on this site, which he purchased from the artist and photographer Peter Beard and his wife, Sheila Teague, that Jack built his house in 1993. Working from the raw bush, Jack orientated his property to take advantage of the summer breezes – the southerly trade winds – rather than the

Opposite: *Like other villas on Mustique, Simplicity has been designed to take advantage of the summer breezes and long, hot days, and every room opens on to a comfortably furnished terrace.*
Above: *Simplicity's location on the Atlantic side of Mustique means that it has wonderful views over the wild and beautiful beach at Pasture Bay.*

considerably stronger easterly winds that blow in around Christmas. Simplicity is a three-bedroomed house with a staff cottage, garden terraces and a swimming pool, designed as a series of separate pavilions, joined by courtyards and pergolas of yellow bougainvillea and trellised thunbergia. Each building takes advantage of the southerly breeze, with panoramic views over the sea. Set apart from the main house, which is built of plastered concrete with painted wooden ceilings, cedar shingle roofs and windows shielded by painted wooden shutters, the pavilions provide privacy for guests, who need meet up with others only once a day.

At the time that Jack was investing time, money and effort in his plot on the wild side of the island, Mustique was undergoing a change in management, and other owners, anxious about its future, sought to keep the place as natural and unspoilt as possible. The Mustique Company was set up to protect the island from exploitation, with a charter controlled by the government of St Vincent and the Grenadines, and all the owners bought shares. The company decreed that there would be no duty payable on building products and materials – which needed to be imported from Barbados or elsewhere – and it produced a masterplan to develop a local building industry. At the same time it established the maximum number of properties sustainable on the island, taking into account the need for green spaces and nature trails between the plots. It was also agreed that, to put off day-trippers, there would be only one small hotel.

The company's initiatives stabilized the island. The airport runway was deliberately made short so that it could not accommodate private jets or commercial airliners. People keen to reach the secluded beaches of Mustique must fly via Barbados and take a small twin-engine plane to

*The understated yet stylish living-room is open on all sides; the furniture is upholstered in simple calico.*

the island. The landing strip closes at dusk and, to discourage mass tourism, casual visitors are charged heavily.

For Jack, Simplicity, overlooking Pasture Bay, is a refuge to which he retreats with his family from his hectic working life in Toronto to do absolutely nothing. The villa is a beach house, where life needs to be simple. In fact, the pace of each day is so much slower than Jack is used to that on arrival he experiences at least forty-eight hours of frustration, until the mood of the island takes him over and he adopts a routine of rest and recuperation, concentrating on himself and his family, including children and grandchildren. His hectic routine is gradually replaced by the construction demands of his grandchildren, for whom he focuses his architectural skills on the creation of state-of-the-art sandcastles on the bone-white coral beaches below the house.

Top left: *A collection of shells and other treasures found on the beach covers a table in the living-room.*
Top right and bottom left: *The master bedroom is attached to the main house, while the two guest bedrooms are separate, each with an inner courtyard, en suite bathroom and outdoor shower.*
Bottom right: *Since most of the day is spent out of doors, the rooms are sparingly furnished.*

# Talaysac

## Gers

### FRANCE

The Gers is a small area of the Midi-Pyrénées region in south-west France. An unacknowledged treasure in the heart of the country, it is today more famous for its garlic and Armagnac than for its wealthy heyday in the eighteenth century, the legacy of which lies in the beautiful *chartreuses* (single-storey houses with basements, characteristic of the area) and ruined chateaux that still dot the landscape. A region that survived centuries of war and the constant threat of invasion has now suffered a different kind of influx: all sorts of foreigners, from well-heeled professionals to penniless adventurers, have been captivated by the ultimate French rural idyll.

One damp weekend in November, a couple staying with French friends in the area found themselves involved in a game whereby the assembled party would attempt to visit in one afternoon as many as possible of the local properties for sale. The local estate agent, who had clearly played

the game several times before, promptly produced a substantial list of houses as candidates. The English clients would doubtless be looking for a property with no running water, no electricity, no roof, and a price tag of less than £20,000.

As one tumbledown property succeeded another, the mood of the pair started to match the weather, until the intrepid estate agent mentioned one final possibility, no sooner uttered than ruled out, since it was certainly no ruin and much too expensive. Human nature being what it is, the couple were immediately curious.

A narrow country lane, potholed and lined with oak copses, wound its way across an undulating landscape of desiccated sunflowers and ploughed fields. A bright-orange setting sun, dispelling the gloom as if by arrangement, shone low through the trees to illuminate a stone-and-terracotta

*Opposite: The garden descends beyond a stone-and-terracotta balustrade and a narrow country lane to a wilderness of trees and an old* bassin *(ornamental pond). An* orangerie, pigeonnier *and other outbuildings complete the* domaine.
Above: *Used throughout the summer, the loggia has curtains made of peasant sheets for extra shade.*

balustrade above the lane and the crumbling façade of a beautiful Italianate manor house. Huge wrought-iron gates, a nineteenth-century *orangerie* in desperate need of repair, outhouses galore, a farmhouse and a *pigeonnier* completed the picture. It was like entering the *domaine* of Alain-Fournier's novel *Le Grand Meaulnes*.

By the end of the weekend, the game had been won once again by the French, the pair had paid a deposit on the manor house, called Talaysac, and a *notaire* had been summoned to complete the paperwork. The couple returned home in a state of numb disbelief at the realization that they were now the owners of a *maison de vacances*, and promptly put their London flat on the market!

Six months after their *folie de grandeur* the couple were knee-deep in stonemasons, plasterers, roofers, plumbers and other helpful artisans, all keen to recommend the correct way to restore Talaysac

Opposite, clockwise from top left: *An old sofa in the summer dining-room has been upholstered in a Majorcan textile, beneath a series of Pompeiian-style prints; a bedroom corner is covered with sketches and watercolours; the study is painted a Chinese red, and one of its walls is lined with elm-wood cupboards; bookcases were built into one wall of the L-shaped upstairs landing.*
Above: *The kitchen ceiling is painted* rouge basque, *which picks up the colour of the original tiles.*

Left: *A rare Turkish kilim covers the floor of the master bedroom. The metal four-poster bed has cotton drapes and is covered in a Victorian patchwork bedspread.*

Top right: *The Victorian bath in the connecting bathroom was found in the garden of a local* brocante.

Bottom right: *A walk-in larder, wine cellar and original laundry area with a stone basin for washing adjoin the vast kitchen and provide essential extra storage.*

and suggest inventive ways of separating them from their hard-earned money. By the time the house was habitable, a pattern had been set whereby, for years to come, the owners spent holidays and snatched weekends painting, decorating and foraging in local *brocantes* (flea markets). They had decided that simplicity should be maintained throughout, with a nod to the Directoire style of the architecture.

In compensation for days of relentless activity, the evenings would be spent in the cool of the terrace, enjoying long, simple suppers washed down by ice-cold local rosé wine. The conversation inevitably focused on the next room to be tackled or an unexpected drainage problem, as well as on how much more the restoration was costing than had been envisaged.

With the house sound and semi-furnished, though still lacking many essentials, in age-old Gers tradition a dinner party was held for the artisans and their wives in the huge kitchen. Using tabletops

improvised from old doors and benches made from leftover planks supported by oil drums, the English couple entertained more than thirty people for a hilarious evening, which ended, many bottles of rosé later, with the stronger and more inebriated of the party attempting to place the stone base and marble top of a table in the living-room. Chaotic directions and gesticulations resulted in the table's phenomenally heavy base being placed upside down at the wrong end of the room; it was some time before it was moved again.

Talaysac was blessed with a remarkable atmosphere and a unique peace, which meant that no one who came to stay left feeling quite the same as when they had arrived. The *domaine* was the focal point of a dream, and some dreams are destined to be shared.

*Tati, an elderly Alsatian dog of unknown origin, arrived quietly one summer and took up residence in the ruined orangerie. Its walls of rustic frescoes and other elements of grandeur were more to his liking than the barn he was offered.*

# Cape Agulhas

## Struisbaai
## Western Cape

SOUTH AFRICA

Cape Agulhas, the southernmost point of Africa, is less than two hours' drive from urban Cape Town, yet it could be a world away. It was named Agulhas ('needles') by Portuguese seafarers, a name that may have been inspired by the ragged and sharp reefs that lie offshore. Cape Agulhas is also officially the point where the Atlantic and Indian oceans meet, in surprisingly shallow waters that are known to provide some of the best fishing grounds in South Africa. Only 145 kilometres (90 miles) north-west of Cape Agulhas lies the Cape of Good Hope, which was referred to by sailors as the 'Cape of Storms', and local folklore is full of stories of shipwrecks.

Struisbaai, a fishing village established on Cape Agulhas in the mid-nineteenth century, recalls life as it used to be on this remote coastline; its whitewashed and thatched fishermen's cottages have been restored as a historical monument. The row of humble properties that makes up the

village overlooks a 14-kilometre (8¾-mile) stretch of sandy beach, above which an impressive lighthouse stands sentinel; dating from 1848, the lighthouse is still operational, and its beacon is visible from at least 50 kilometres (31 miles) away.

This stretch of coast has recently seen a new arrival in the shape of a modern vacation home built unapologetically on a windswept rocky promontory. The well-travelled owner discovered the plot by chance one weekend as she was driving along the coast. It took her two years to refine her plans and, with the help of her son and a young architect, Stefan Antoni, to create the house of her dreams.

Set between the ocean and the mountains, the building is regularly at the mercy of mighty winds and other severe weather conditions, but its position protects it from the very worst storms. It is sheltered on the landward side by a low incline, which also prevents the house from dominating or

*The low-lying contemporary building, set on a remote promontory between the ocean and the mountains, has an open terrace that faces away from the sea and is thereby protected from the prevailing wind.*

Constructed in glass and natural materials, such as local sandstone and wood, the house has been designed to take advantage of its unique yet vulnerable setting, and the distinctions between outside and inside are successfully blurred.

spoiling its immediate environment. For the owner, whose childhood was spent in Egypt, and who has had an intimate relationship with the sea throughout her life, one of the main attractions of this remote and wild place was its proximity to the ocean and to nature. Only a thin strip of *fynbos* (the shrubby vegetation of this stretch of coast) separates the property from the ocean, and the sound of the waves is alternately gentle and resounding, filling the house as soon as a window is opened. The surf erupts against a line of dark, serrated rocks below, leaving a canopy of gleaming brown kelp exposed on the shoreline, while seabirds duck and dive on the air currents.

After a storm, the owner combs the alcoves along the beach for fine-veined nautilus shells and other natural treasures that can be found almost intact, left by the receding tide. Despite her family's amused objections, she has decorated every spare surface in the house with her spoils.

The property has neither hallway nor corridors but consists mainly of a large open-plan room that includes a kitchen area, dining area and sitting area. This main space opens on to bedrooms and bathrooms that have windows that slide back into the walls, allowing occupants the luxury of bathing under the stars. Everyone who comes to stay lends a hand with the cooking and cleaning. Visitors spend much of the day on the vast terrace, where they can take a siesta in hammocks when not walking in the surrounding nature reserve and bird sanctuary or exploring the shoreline beneath the house.

Wonderful for entertaining, the property is equally cosy when the owner stays there alone. She often spends weeks at a time content in her own company, but admits that since building the house she and her family have acquired many new friends.

Left: *The modern, simple master bedroom has sliding windows that open towards the sea.*
Top right: *The ceiling of the main room drops down over the sitting area to create an intimate and comfortable space in which to relax.*
Bottom right: *All the rooms, including the bedrooms and this bathroom with its sunken bath, have windows that slide back into the walls, opening them to the sea and the sky.*

# Podere Zingoni

## Val d'Orcia · Tuscany

ITALY

Considered to be one of the most beautiful regions in Italy, Tuscany is characterized by a landscape of gently rolling hills dotted with pole-straight cypress trees, often flanking dusty farm tracks that lead to isolated stone buildings. The region's matchless artistic heritage encompasses architecture, painting and sculpture, and, in addition, the countryside is wonderfully varied and unspoilt, its fields of corn alternating with vineyards and row upon row of sunflowers. Small wonder, then, that Tuscany is so popular with Italians and foreigners alike, many of whom scour the region for abandoned farmhouses to convert into vacation homes.

Ilaria and Giorgio Miani first discovered Podere Zingoni in the early 1990s, at a time when they had already bought and restored two other ruins in the nearby town of San Casciano dei Bagni. Perched on a ridge, Podere Zingoni has a beautiful garden that descends through a series of

Page 212: *Dinner is often enjoyed by the light of twinkling lanterns in the garden.*
Previous page: *The house offers magnificent views over the surrounding countryside.*
Above: *Seen from the terrace, the breathtaking landscape is framed like a series of paintings by the poles of the pergola.*
Opposite: *The sitting-room has comfortable chairs covered in bright fabrics to complement the bold paint effect that Ilaria has used throughout the house.*

terraces redolent of rosemary, thyme and other fragrant herbs. It was one of several properties that the Mianis bought in the Val d'Orcia, and certainly not the last. The couple readily admit that they are obsessed with Tuscany and are always buying neglected properties to restore; at the last count they had eight.

Based in Rome, the Mianis divide their time during the week in practical fashion, with Giorgio working on the restoration of the Tuscan villas and Ilaria running her design showroom in the capital city. When they started to restore Tuscan farmhouses more than twenty years ago, it became evident that they would not find the necessary fixtures and furniture in local antiques shops. Ever resourceful, Ilaria set about designing and manufacturing everything for her properties, from canopy beds to accessories. So successful was the enterprise that she now sells from her shop in Rome

Top left: *Pale lemon and grey are the dominant colours in the hall.*
Right: *The kitchen is painted raspberry and teal. Open shelves are used to store pots, pans and crockery.*
Bottom left: *A bench covered with cushions occupies a corner of the dining-room. The two prints of horses were bought in London.*

ranges of furniture handmade in Tuscany by local craftsmen. Giorgio and Ilaria come together at weekends, spending what they describe as 'special time' in Tuscany, entertaining friends and family at their house, Buonriposo, and using nearby Podere Zingoni as a guest house.

Podere Zingoni is at the end of a dirt track, an isolated stone-built farmhouse that, in spite of its apparently small size, has five bedrooms. The couple have kept the original structure, but on the ground floor, which would originally have been divided into animal stalls, rooms have been opened up and windows added to let in light. Upstairs, they have installed bathrooms while respecting the graceful proportions of the original rooms.

As an interior designer, Ilaria is conscious that time and use can give houses a tired look. Much of the structural work at Podere Zingoni was carried out in the early 1990s, so she decided recently

to refresh its interior decoration. Seeking to preserve a sense of the house's simple origins as a peasant dwelling, she has modernized it with great sensitivity. The consummate hostess, Ilaria likes to keep the decoration and furnishing of her houses as flexible and 'free' as possible, so that rooms can be changed to suit the mood of the moment or to accommodate guests at short notice.

Apart from its glorious isolation and fabulous views over the undulating countryside, there are plenty of reasons for guests to be attracted to Podere Zingoni. Mornings are typically spent relaxing beside the slate-grey swimming pool, with lunch and local wine served on one of the garden terraces, followed by a long siesta or a gentle walk in the late afternoon, before the day draws to a close in the shade of a vine-hung pergola. Why would anyone in their right mind wish to leave this haven of peace and tranquility to join the *autostrada* back to Rome?

Top and bottom left: *Each of these three bedrooms is decorated in Ilaria's idiosyncratic style, with bold colours and bright textiles.*
Bottom right: *This simple bathroom has a bold stripe of deep red running around the walls.*

# Cill Rialaig

## County Kerry

IRELAND

A mere cluster of tiny stone cottages, Cill Rialaig in County Kerry, one of the westernmost points of habitation in Europe, clings to the edge of the cliff on Bolus Head high above the Atlantic Ocean and Ballinskelligs Bay. Built around 1790, and exposed over the centuries to the relentless pounding of the elements, the eleven cottages that make up this isolated hamlet have suffered a heavy toll.

The surrounding landscape is beautiful, rugged and demanding. The rocky terrain and spectacular cliffs, with views of Scariff Island and the distant Skelligs, resonate with the mysticism that in previous centuries encouraged many to seek out this wild, unforgiving countryside and endure there a daily battle for survival. A line of megaliths leading up to Bolus Head and the ruins of a hermitage beyond the village stand testimony to those who have gone before. There are also survivors from the days when Cill Rialaig was still a struggling community. Mrs Kelly, the last person

to vacate the hamlet, in the 1950s, now lives in a modern bungalow as close as possible to her old home, which, like many of the other cottages, finally descended into ruin. Yet from the luxury of her new surroundings Mrs Kelly has witnessed the previously unthinkable: the extraordinary restoration of her village by Noelle Campbell-Sharp, a successful publisher from Dublin, under the sensitive stewardship of the architect Alfred Cochrane.

The latest chapter in Cill Rialaig's history began when Noelle first visited the area in the late 1980s and, like many before her, was captivated by the spectacular scenery and the stubborn tenacity of its inhabitants. Not far from the hamlet, she bought a pair of old ruined cottages and a cowshed from two elderly sisters, who agreed to sell only after she had promised to respect in her restoration the buildings' simple vernacular architecture.

Opposite: *The slate-roofed cottage, one of the first of the hamlet's eleven cottages to have been restored, is located on the cliffs of the Iveragh Peninsula above the wild shores of County Kerry, overlooking the Atlantic Ocean.*
Above: *A peat fire burns next to a small cast-iron stove in Noelle's own cosy sitting-room.*

Above, left: *Bare stone walls are a feature of Noelle's restored cottage, which is a very short distance from the hamlet of Cill Rialaig.*
Above, right: *The sitting-room in the adjoining cottage is less rustic, but also has a peat fire, in a more conventional fireplace.*
Opposite: *One wall of the ground-floor sitting-room contains what locals refer to as 'keeping holes', used for housing books. A ladder leads up to a small loft. On the rustic table is a collection of Iveragh ceramics by Bob Hollis.*

To link the cowshed with the two cottages and to devise a means of honouring Noelle's pledge, Alfred erected a conservatory – known as the 'sky room' – between the two buildings, keeping the original stone walls of both properties and incorporating the irregularities of each into the overall design. The glazed conservatory roof ensures that the room is bathed in any available sunshine, in contrast to the dark and cosy sitting-room, which has small windows under a low thatch.

As Noelle's own house began to take shape, she became increasingly involved with the local community, eventually coming up with the idea of rekindling life in the abandoned clifftop village. With the help of friends, a small National Lottery grant and a wealth of enthusiasm, Noelle bought the collection of tumbledown cottages in 1991 and, with Alfred, has been restoring them ever since.

Noelle's bedroom is decorated in shades of pale blue. A rustic patchwork quilt covers the bed, swirling blue watercolours adorn the walls, and pale Indian saris filter the northern light that streams in through the small windows.

Two cottages have been completed, one thatched and the other with a slate roof, standing on opposite sides of the steep rutted track that climbs up to Cill Rialaig. Constructed of hard-wearing concrete blocks clad with the original stones, each cottage has a skylight hidden from view behind a false raised-brick chimney. A peat-burning stove is positioned where the original back wall of the cottage and chimney-breast would have been. The sleeping accommodation is a simple platform approached by a steep ladder against a wall of 'keeping holes'. Progress on the overall project is slow, however, since restoration is so much more expensive than new building, and the remaining nine cottages have a long way to go before being habitable.

Noelle has set out to create a new artistic community at Cill Rialaig, drawing on the unique spirit of the hamlet to attract artists and writers to spend a month at a time in relative isolation in one of

the cottages, where they can work and sleep without being disturbed. In exchange for this unusual accommodation, which is offered without charge, a tradition has been established whereby visiting artists leave behind something that they have produced during the month of their stay; the artwork can then be sold to raise funds. The idea has proved extremely popular, and the unique quality of light in this far-flung outpost of Ireland has attracted artists of international repute.

Left: *In a bedroom with an iron bedstead, the bedroom and cupboard doors have been painted in a matching pattern; there is a similar brightly painted cupboard in the bathroom.*

Top right: *The blue-painted, late-Victorian fireplace in Noelle's bedroom is another elegant and decorative feature of this isolated cottage.*

Bottom right: *The guest bedroom is also dominated by an iron bedstead; the length of local fabric on the wall behind adds a sense of grandeur.*

# Casa Luna

## Careyes Bay
## Puerto Vallarta

MEXICO

Costa Careyes in Mexico is a luxury development of multicoloured villas and beautiful houses erupting like variegated mushrooms on the cliffs overlooking the Pacific Ocean between Puerto Vallarta and Manzanillo. Spied from a small plane in the late 1960s by Gian Franco Brignone, an Italian financier, the 13-kilometre (8-mile) stretch of land was to start with little more than a cluster of lagoons and small bays, with few towns, no electricity supply, no roads and no airport.

Since then Gian Franco has devoted his life to developing this stretch of coast, reputedly the most beautiful in Mexico, in what he believes to be the best way possible. He commissioned two Mexican architects to build a handful of brightly painted Mexican-style bungalows, or *casitas*, thereby laying the foundations of a vacation Utopia.

Pages 224–25: *Casa Luna is built on a beautiful but restricted site, cleared by the house's architect, Manolo Mestre, who wanted to give the impression of multiple spaces and views.*
Above, clockwise from top left: *A monolithic stone fountain, inspired by old fonts, is sheltered by a pink wall; a hammock hangs between two palm trees; chiselled or polished cement floors provide different textures throughout the house, and the entrance is emphasized with stained tree trunks; the living area's comfortable furniture was designed by the architect.*

The area has since been designated a protected ecological zone, where hawksbill and loggerhead turtles return every winter to lay their eggs on the shore. Gian Franco's love of horses means that there is a stable of sixty animals, as well as two polo fields and miles of trails and empty beaches of white sand for riding. This haven is well known among the international jet-set and those who inhabit the world of high fashion, but apparently by few others. To those 'in the know', Careyes – a combination of privately owned villas and *casitas*, some available for rent, and a single hotel, El Careyes Beach Resort – is a laid-back alternative to other resorts around the world, where media focus continues to be a daily intrusion.

The affluent international crowd is attracted by the fact that there is no town to speak of, and no nightclubs or glitzy boutiques. Instead, visitors prefer to relax around the infinity pools and open-

air living spaces of these exceptional properties, coming together in the evenings for candlelit parties. Privacy is guaranteed, and for those drawn to the simple luxury of Costa Careyes and its Playa Rosa, this appears to be, whatever the cost, something worth paying for.

A few more villas have been added to this extraordinary place over the years, but there is no impression of overcrowding, and it is rare to glimpse another visitor on the cobbled streets that coil around the lushly planted hillside properties. The Mexican architect Manolo Mestre has been involved in the design of several new villas. Careyes is one of his favourite places because of its wonderful sense of unity, and everything he has built there is characterized by an explosion of colour.

Casa Luna, designed as a home for an American family who wished to divide their time between Los Angeles and Mexico, offered a blank canvas for the imaginative architect. Looking out

*A curved, white-upholstered banquette punctuated with a liberal scattering of brightly coloured, textured cushions makes a comfortable area in which to relax in the shade of the palapa.*

*Inside the villa, striking red and orange walls, pillars, floors and stairs emphasize the modern, sculptural quality of the architecture. The pots that decorate the entrance hall were found in the local village.*

over the Pacific Ocean, the villa is designed to wrap around the hillside behind it. Its interior is contemporary, clean and colourful, with furniture that Manolo designed and had made by local craftsmen. Casa Luna exemplifies his strong belief that Mexican design is destined to return to simple, natural materials, raw stones and hand-carved wood.

The house, like each of the properties Manolo has created in this Mexican idyll, has been designed around a *palapa*, a massive thatched roof that soars above all the open-air living areas. The design incorporates a modern interpretation of traditional Mexican stucco in the form of concrete polished as smooth as marble and then rendered in bright pastels. Inspired by objects that have a soul, such as pottery and folk art from Central and South America, Manolo likes to adapt vernacular styles and materials to suit each location, rather than being influenced by fashion.

Now in his eighties, Gian Franco has set up schools and a health service for the local people in Careyes, as well as providing an opportunity for ecologically aware members of the jet-set to lose themselves, albeit temporarily, in an exclusive but simple paradise. His dream was to create a Utopia where social standing would be measured by eccentricity and the knowledge gained from travel in far-flung lands rather than by extravagant yachts. His 'guests' and those who rent the villas and casitas can now land at the small airport that he has built at Manzanillo. Tourism, as such, is discouraged, so only those who are determined to make it to the Playa Rosa get through.

*The bed platform and the painted surrounds for the window- and door frames are picked out in blue, while the emphasis in the sculpted bathroom is on a subtle shade of pink. Manolo believes in 'tactile architecture', so all the cement floors are designed to feel good under bare feet.*

# Wolter House

## Gordes · Vaucluse

FRANCE

Ted Wolter is one of life's travellers. As his skills as a jewellery designer evolved, he developed a peripatetic lifestyle that took him from Canada, where he grew up, to Mexico, Santa Fe, Florence and the South of France, and he has owned shops in Manhattan, Washington, D.C., and East Hampton. During the past few years Ted has divided his time between Santa Fe and Provence, where in 2000 he began transforming a charming house outside Gordes into a second home.

Gordes is a beautiful village perched on the southern edge of the high Plateau de Vaucluse, and its approach through terraces of ancient olive trees is reputed to be one of the most spectacular in the region. Its stone houses and impressive Renaissance castle cluster on the side of the cliff, with views to the distant mountains of the Lubéron, 40 kilometres (25 miles) east of Avignon. Gordes itself has become a tourist honeypot, but Ted's house is in the nearby countryside, amid vineyards.

Ted originally heard about the house through friends who were antiques dealers in the area. His first visit was discouraging, revealing an empty property that had not been lived in for several years. The only things left to salvage were some broken items of farm machinery. There was no garden, no gravel; only one dead tree in the centre of the courtyard. However, he soon realized that the house's advantages far outweighed its deficiencies. Its stone walls and terracotta-tiled roof date from the sixteenth century, and some parts of the property are even older, but, apart from the addition of French windows in the living-room and dining area, few structural changes were necessary.

The traditional houses in the region have thick walls and the windows are kept small as protection against the mistral, the wind that 'tows a melancholy brooding in its wake' the length of France's south coast. Ted retained the small windows, resisting the impulse common to many who

Left and top right: *Secure within its tranquil courtyard, this house on the outskirts of Gordes is surrounded by vineyards.*

Bottom right: *A modern French limestone table with canvas-and-wood chairs from Ted's shop, Lucca & Co, takes pride of place in the summer dining area.*

move to a foreign country to introduce architectural elements that are out of harmony with the local climate and conditions. Interestingly, he took his influence from The Netherlands (where, historically, small windows helped to retain heat) and shrouded the interior of his French home in cool shadow.

The curved, vaulted ceiling of the living-room was replastered and the floor covered with eighteenth-century tiles. The kitchen was enhanced with a nineteenth-century French shop counter, while the other rooms in the house benefited from spare groupings of furniture, mainly sourced in Italy and France. Ted has never regarded furniture as particularly important in itself. For him, what counts is comfort and clarity. So, while the rooms are scantily furnished, the house is both welcoming and surprising.

Ted spends little time these days at his house in France, but when he does drop by, normally with a friend or two, he is easily seduced into shopping sprees at the antiques market in nearby

Opposite: *A sofa draped in Irish linen makes a good spot for relaxing in the summer dining area.* Above, left and top right: *The work surface in the kitchen is made of Belgian stone and is supplemented by an antique French shop counter. Glasses and crockery are stored on open shelves.* Above, bottom right: *A simple flight of stone steps leads up to the first floor.*

L'Isle-sur-la-Sorgue. Otherwise, he is content to while away the hours of daylight reading in the shade of the terrace or walking his dog through the neighbouring olive groves in the cool of early evening. With Uzès, Marseilles and Nice all an easy car journey away, Ted's quest for antiques can be quickly fulfilled, while L'Isle-sur-la-Sorgue has several cafés and restaurants that he likes to visit with friends.

Ted's one regret about his house in Gordes is its lack of a proper garden. He has recently remedied this gap in his life with the purchase of a 60.5-hectare (150-acre) farm in Italy, including a farmhouse that will no doubt acquire the same mix of spareness and comfort as his French retreat. He admits to being minimalist by nature, taking very little of material value with him when he moves from place to place.

Opposite: *The chimneypiece in the sparsely furnished living-room is original to the house. The long, low cocktail table is by Jerome Abel Seguin.*
Above, left and top right: *Objects on display in the guest bedroom include eighteenth-century prints on the walls and an antique African terracotta pot on the mantelpiece.*
Above, bottom right: *The master bedroom has an eighteenth-century chair and a French Empire mirror on the mantelpiece. Irish linen covers the bed.*

# Design Directory

**Stefan Antoni**
Stefan Antoni Olmesdahl Truen Architects
109 Hatfield Street
Gardens
Cape Town, 8001
South Africa
+27 21 4222 406
info@saota.com; saota.com

**Ou Baholyodhin**
Unit 2C, 9–15 Elthorne Road
London N19 6AJ
+44 (0)20 7272 2272
ou@ou-b.com; ou-b.com

**Liza Bruce**
9 Pont Street
London SW1X 9EJ
+44 (0)20 7235 8423
info@lizabruce.com; lizabruce.com

**Alfred Cochrane**
Alfrank Designs
Unit 730, Kilshane Drive
Dublin 15
Ireland
+353 1 8091402
alfrank.ie

**Jasper Conran**
36 Sackville Street
London W1S 3EQ
+44 (0)20 7292 9080
sackvillestore@jasperconran.com; jasperconran.com

**John and Monique Davidson (J&M Davidson)**
42 Ledbury Road
Notting Hill
London W11 2AB
+44 (0)20 7313 9532
info@jandm-davidson.co.uk; jandmdavidson.com

**Jack Diamond**
Diamond + Schmitt Architects
384 Adelaide Street West, Suite 300
Toronto
Canada M5V 1R7
+1 416 862 8800
info@dsai.ca; dsai.ca

**Peter Dunham**
909 North Orlando Avenue
Los Angeles, CA 90069
USA
+1 323 848 9900
PeterDLA@aol.com; peterdunham.com

**Kirsten Hecktermann**
+44 (0)7887 680672
info@kirstenhecktermann.com;
kirstenhecktermann.com

**Kathryn Ireland**
1619 Stanford Street
Santa Monica, CA 90404
USA
+1 310 315 4351
info@kathrynireland.com; kathrynireland.com

**Menno Meinesz**
+27 (0)11 726 8257

**Ilaria Miani**
Via Monserrato 35
00186 Rome
+39 06 683 3160
ilariamiani.it

**Jacqueline Morabito**
42, rue Yves Klein
06480 La Colle-sur-Loup
France
+33 (0)4 93 32 64 92
jm@jacquelinemorabito.com;
jacquelinemorabito.com

# Vacation Homes to Rent

**Paco Muñoz**
Calle Sol 58 bajo
46910 Alfafar
Valencia
Spain
+34 96 117 59 10
info@pacomunyoz.com; pacomunyoz.com

**Mimmi O'Connell**
8 Eaton Square
London SW1W 9DB
+44 (0)20 7752 0474
mimmi.oconnell@googlemail.com;
mimmioconnell.com

**Carolyn Quartermaine**
+44 (0)20 7373 4492
info@carolynquartermaine.com;
carolynquartermaine.com

**Beach House**
Shela House Management Ltd
PO Box 439
Lamu – 80500
Kenya
+ 254 (0)42 633419
shela@africaonline.co.ke; shelahouse.com

**La Casa de la Palmera**
brenda.hartill@gmail.com; palmeratravel.co.uk

**Château de Moissac**
Available as a location.
Marie-Christine Cavaglione: +33 607 393 709

**Dunton Hot Springs**
P.O. Box 818
Dolores, CO 81323
USA
+1 970 882 4800
info@duntonhotsprings.com;
duntonhotsprings.com

**The Glen**
Can be rented for three or four weeks in June
or July each year.
aastor@okadirect.com

**La Herrumbrossa**
visiontarifa.com

**Podere Zingoni**
giorgiomiani@tin.it; ilariamiani.it

**Quartermaine House**
Available as a location.
carolynquartermaine@hotmail.com

**Simplicity**
simplicitymustique.com;
jackandgillian@hotmail.com

**Tangala**
+260 99 312766
reservations@tongabezi.com; tongabezi.com

**Tizac**
tizac.tarn@yahoo.com

**Tounis**
lacastellane.com

**Vygekraal**
+27 11 807 1800
castleonthecliff.com

## Acknowledgements

With grateful thanks to:
Tim Beddow
Michael Boodro
Sally Brampton
Kate Constable
Patricia Daunt
Elizabeth Helman Minchilli
Giles Kime
Ed Lanfranco
Vicky Lowry
Celia Lyttelton
Nonie Nieswand
Christine Pittel
Elfreda Pownall
Anthony Roberts
Matthew Shaw

## Picture Credits

Photographic agency The Interior Archive, owned by Karen Howes, is extremely fortunate to work exclusively with a group of internationally renowned interiors photographers, without whom this beautiful book would not have been possible. Grateful thanks are extended to each contributor.

Bill Batten: pp. 156–59.
Tim Beddow (timbeddow.com): pp. 32–43, 50–55, 128–33, 170–75, 184–87.
Nicolas Bruant: pp. 150–55.
Jacques Dirand: pp. 84–89.
Mark Luscombe-Whyte (markluscombewhyte.com): front cover, back cover (top left), pp. 114–19, 176–83, 224–29, 239.
Simon McBride (currently with Red Cover): back cover (bottom right), pp. 218–23.
Simon Upton (simonupton.com): pp. 62–65, 94–99, 104–13, 134–37, 188–91, 212–17, 230–38.
Fritz von der Schulenburg (fritzvonderschulenburg.com): back cover (top right and bottom left) pp. 4, 16–27, 44–49, 56–61, 66–83, 90–93, 100–103, 120–27, 138–49, 160–69, 192–97, 202–11.
Luke White (lukewhite.com): pp. 28–31, 198–201

First published 2007 by
Merrell Publishers Limited

Head office
81 Southwark Street
London SE1 0HX

New York office
49 West 24th Street, 8th Floor
New York, NY 10010

merrellpublishers.com

Text, design and layout copyright © 2007
Merrell Publishers Limited
Illustrations copyright © 2007 The Interior
Archive Limited

British Library Cataloguing-in-Publication Data:
Howes, Karen
Vacation homes and perfect weekend hideaways
1. Vacation homes 2. Interior decoration
I. Title
728.7'2

ISBN-13: 978-1-8589-4369-5
ISBN-10: 1-8589-4369-8

Produced by Merrell Publishers Limited
Designed by Martin Lovelock
Copy-edited by Henrietta Heald
Proof-read by Vanessa Bird

Printed and bound in China

Front cover image: Watts–Gurney House, Australia, pp. 114–19
Back cover images, clockwise from top left: Casa Luna, Mexico, pp. 224–29; Beach House, Kenya, pp. 138–43; Cill Rialaig, Ireland, pp. 218–23; Dunton Hot Springs, USA, pp. 120–27
Page 4: Ocean View, St Vincent and the Grenadines, pp. 44–49
Page 238: Podere Zingoni, Italy, pp. 212–17
Page 239: Casa Luna, Mexico, pp. 224–29